W9-AYE-666

TRANSGRESSIONS: CULTURAL STUDIES AND EDUCATION
Volume 60

TRANSGRESSIONS: CULTURAL STUDIES AND EDUCATION

Cultural studies provides an analytical toolbox for both making sense of educational practice and extending the insights of educational professionals into their labors. In this context *Transgressions: Cultural Studies and Education* provides a collection of books in the domain that specify this assertion. Crafted for an audience of teachers, teacher educators, scholars and students of cultural studies and others interested in cultural studies and pedagogy, the series documents both the possibilities of and the controversies surrounding the intersection of cultural studies and education. The editors and the authors of this series do not assume that the interaction of cultural studies and education devalues other types of knowledge and analytical forms. Rather the intersection of these knowledge disciplines offers a rejuvenating, optimistic, and positive perspective on education and educational institutions. Some might describe its contribution as democratic, emancipatory, and transformative. The editors and authors maintain that cultural studies helps free educators from sterile, monolithic analyses that have for too long undermined efforts to think of educational practices by providing other words, new languages, and fresh metaphors. Operating in an interdisciplinary cosmos, Transgressions: Cultural Studies and Education is dedicated to exploring the ways cultural studies enhances the study and practice of education. With this in mind the series focuses in a non-exclusive way on popular culture as well as other dimensions of cultural studies including social theory, social justice and positionality, cultural dimensions of technological innovation, new media and media literacy, new forms of oppression emerging in an electronic hyperreality, and postcolonial global concerns. With these concerns in mind cultural studies scholars often argue that the realm of popular culture is the most powerful educational force in contemporary culture. Indeed, in the twenty-first century this pedagogical dynamic is sweeping through the entire world. Educators, they believe, must understand these emerging realities in order to gain an important voice in the pedagogical conversation.

Without an understanding of cultural pedagogy's (education that takes place outside of formal schooling) role in the shaping of individual identity–youth identity in particular–the role educators play in the lives of their students will continue to fade. Why do so many of our students feel that life is incomprehensible and devoid of meaning? What does it mean, teachers wonder, when young people are unable to describe their moods, their affective affiliation to the society around them. Meanings provided young people by mainstream institutions often do little to help them deal with their affective complexity, their difficulty negotiating the rift between meaning and affect. School knowledge and educational expectations seem as anachronistic as a ditto machine, not that learning ways of rational thought and making sense of the world are unimportant.

But school knowledge and educational expectations often have little to offer students about making sense of the way they feel, the way their affective lives are shaped. In no way do we argue that analysis of the production of youth in an electronic mediated world demands some "touchy-feely" educational superficiality. What is needed in this context is a rigorous analysis of the interrelationship between pedagogy, popular culture, meaning making, and youth subjectivity. In an era marked by youth depression, violence, and suicide such insights become extremely important, even life saving. Pessimism about the future is the common sense of many contemporary youth with its concomitant feeling that no one can make a difference.

If affective production can be shaped to reflect these perspectives, then it can be reshaped to lay the groundwork for optimism, passionate commitment, and transformative educational and political activity. In these ways cultural studies adds a dimension to the work of education unfilled by any other sub-discipline. This is what Transgressions: Cultural Studies and Education seeks to produce—literature on these issues that makes a difference. It seeks to publish studies that help those who work with young people, those individuals involved in the disciplines that study children and youth, and young people themselves improve their lives in these bizarre times.

Memories of Paulo

Edited by

Tom Wilson
Chapman University, California, USA

Peter Park
University of Massachusetts, USA and Fielding Graduate University, Calafornia, USA

Anaida Colón-Muñiz
Chapman University, California, USA

SENSE PUBLISHERS
ROTTERDAM / TAIPEI

A C.I.P. record for this book is available from the Library of Congress.

ISBN: 978-94-6091-217-7 (paperback)
ISBN: 978-94-6091-218-4 (hardback)
ISBN: 978-94-6091-219-1 (e-book)

Published by: Sense Publishers,
P.O. Box 21858,
3001 AW Rotterdam,
The Netherlands
http://www.sensepublishers.com

Printed on acid-free paper

. . the necessary process from ingenuous to critical curiosity should also be accompanied by a rigorous ethical formation side by side with an aesthetic appreciation.

    –   From Pedagogy of Freedom

Maybe one of the best ways for conceiving of education is to say that it cannot accomplish it all, but it can accomplish something. That is, our problem, of educators, is to ask ourselves if it possible to make viable what sometimes does not seem possible.

    –   From Daring to Dream: A Pedagogy of the Unfinished

DEDICATION

This book of Memories of Paulo Freire is dedicated to Joe Kincheloe (*December 14, 1950–December 19, 2008)*, who truly lived in the spirit of Freire towards a more just society through democratic and liberatory education, and to Bob Howard (*March 22, 1954–April 11, 2010)*, whose tenacious advocacy for just and democratic schooling will never be forgotten.

TABLE OF CONTENTS

TABLE OF CONTENTS

PREFACE

It is always a great honor to be asked on this historical occasion to write a Preface to this important book that brilliantly captures memories of Paulo Freire as recorded by those whose lives he profoundly touched and transformed. At the same time, to read and reread the wonderful recollections that people so dearly hold of Paulo Freire filled me with a complexity of emotions. On the one hand, these often moving and insightful stories bear witness that Paulo Freire lives on and is very much with us and, on the other hand, this book project reconfirms the presence of his absence–an absence that I almost feel daily *com muita mágoa*, with much sadness and pain.

In fact, the reading and rereading of *Memories of Paulo* painfully reminds us of the absence of an exceptional human being who, while he is no longer here with us *em corpo e osso*, he is ever more present in our lives in spirit, generosity, and love. Paulo always talked about the importance of having an enormous capacity to love in order to carry out the arduous and often difficult task of denouncing the cruel and obscene assaults against human beings who have the least when it is so much easier and comfortable to accommodate to the power structure from which we can reap benefits. Paulo exemplified his great capacity to love by the coherence with which he lived his life, and his unyielding commitment to social justice which gave and continues to give all of us tremendous hope that a discriminatory world can be changed to become more just, less dehumanizing, and more humane, acknowledging always that "change is difficult but it is possible." I feel extremely privileged for having known Paulo, for having learned from him what it means to be human, and for having shared many laughs with him and Nita. These memorable moments I shared with Paulo always exhumed hope in his refusal to give up, in his rejection of cynicism, and his total negation of fatalism–a posture that refuses to accept any form of determinism while inviting us to embrace history as possibility. It is a posture that Paulo had in the world and with the world that continues to teach us the meaning of imagining otherwise *para que possamos ser mais* so that we can be more in our humanity. Paulo was a special friend, an exquisite human being, a lovingly militant intellectual whose death leaves a turbulent emptiness in our hearts. At the same time, his passion and compassion will always guide and define our collective struggle to eradicate hatred as we embrace what he always and kindly shared with us: LOVE.

It is within this context of love that *Memories of Paulo* became a reality to the extent that even those who have not consciously acknowledged this fact about Paulo, cannot escape the factor love as they reinvent Paulo in their unending struggle against social injustices, hatred, and all forms of dehumanization. It is the ever-present capacity to love and be loved that inspired, reinvigorated, and re-energized Paulo to share his always brilliant and insightful understanding of the world through the writing of penetrating and unveiling words during the last ten years of his life–words compact with passion, compassion, and wisdom that would perhaps not been written in his last ten years of life without the presence of Nita Freire, who was simultaneously his dedicated *companheira*, student, teacher, and lover since, according to Paulo, "Nita taught him how to love again."

Many of us feared that the death of Elza had cracked the very foundation of Paulo's idealism which had not only attracted us to him and his writings but had also motivated many of us to embrace his challenge to make this world, in his own words, more beautiful, less ugly, more democratic, and less inhumane. Many of us also feared that Paulo had lost his *joie de vivre*, his intense desire to be in the world, to critically comprehend the world so as be able to transform it.

In the winter of 1987, I visited São Paulo to see Paulo, hoping to begin again our collaborative work that had stretched for many years. I remember perfectly the long plane trip from Boston to São Paulo–a trip filled with doubts, fears, and much uncertainty. On the one hand, I wanted desperately to see Paulo and resume our usual and always warm conviviality. On the other hand, I was afraid I would no longer find in Paulo's beautiful and penetrating eyes the vibrancy that had so marked his ways of being in the world and with the world. I did not want to see Paulo without his unyielding belief in utopia that lovingly rejected determinism in favor of embracing history as possibility. I arrived in São Paulo in the morning and I immediately telephoned Paulo. My initial hesitation disappeared almost completely when Paulo's voice beamed with energy and joy. Even though I was very tired from the twelve-hour trip, Paulo insisted that I come to his house for lunch. As usual, I accepted since it was always difficult to say no to Paulo's generous and loving invitations.

When I arrived at his house, Paulo introduced me to a very beautiful, almost classical woman who I thought was his colleague at the university. In introducing her to me, he spoke almost passionately about "her fantastic contributions to the Brazilian history of education," her superb intuition, and her superior capacity for critical analysis. When we sat at the table to have lunch, I felt a great joy to see Paulo again happy. I noticed his insistence that this attractive, elegant, and eloquent woman sit next to him. In fact, in a classic Paulo Freire's loving way, he strategically ushered me to another seat so Nita could be next to him. During this memorable lunch, I realized once again that Paulo always maintained a great coherence between his words, deeds, and ideas. I vividly remembered during that afternoon something that Paulo had shared with me many years earlier: "Never let the child in you die!" His playful gesture toward Nita, his loving smile, his undivided attention while she was explaining her thesis to us, the frequent gaze, and his almost nervous attempt to hold her hands (which he tried many times and not always successfully), made me want to imagine him as a teenager in love.

Many years later and sadly the last time I was with Paulo only months before his untimely death, as he and I were walking in New York, we finally talked about the concern that many of us had felt regarding his lack of desire to live after Elza's death. I told him how happy I was to see him again filled with joy, renewed by an incredible hope, able to dream and love again. I remember clearly when he stopped, turned slightly toward me, and put his hand on my shoulder and said softly: "Yes, Donaldo. I was also fearful that I did not want to live anymore. What

Nita gave me was fantastic, magical! She not only made me rediscover the joy of life but she also taught me a great lesson that I intellectually knew but, somehow, I emotionally could no longer remember: to always view and embrace history as possibility. It is possible to love again."

As we walked on Lexington Avenue, Paulo stopped again and said:

Nita not only taught me that it is possible to love again, but she gave me a new and renewed intellectual energy. I feel re-energized intellectually. For example, my new books, *Pedagogy of Hope* and *Letters to Christina,* could not have been written without her. She not only gave me the intellectual energy, but she also impressed upon me the importance of revisiting my earlier ideas so as to reinvent them. Her keen understanding of history enabled her to make compelling arguments concerning the importance of rethinking those historical contexts that had radicalized my thinking and that had given birth to *Pedagogy of the Oppressed.* Her important notes to these books gave readers an important insight into the historical conditions that made me the thinker, the writer that I am today. This is fantastic! Nita is without a doubt one of the few people who truly and completely understand my work. It is almost scary. Sometimes I think she understands my ideas better than I do.

I would add that without Nita, we would not have *Pedagogy of Freedom,* a book that both Henry Giroux and Stanley Aronowitz consider as one of his best. Without Nita we would not have *Pedagogy of Indignation.* Without Nita we would not have *Pedagogy of Tolerance* and without Nita we would not have *Daring to Dream* and *Pedagogy of Commitment.* Simply put, without Nita we would not have the highly prolific Paulo Freire during his last ten years in this world. We would have an unfinished Paulo Freire who, even is his *unfinishedness,* would still have remained a great Paulo Freire. With Nita's love, dedication, and inspiration, Paulo Freire became more than great. He became the most important educator of the last fifty years in the world. For her uncompromising dedication to Paulo, for her unyielding love to him, and for the loving companionship with him to be more together as soul mates and as intellectuals, we want to collectively say OBRIGADA.

The writing of this Preface to *Memories of Paulo* not only gave me the opportunity to humbly add vivid memories to this important collection of stories that both redefine and reinvent Paulo Freire, but it also allowed me to share with the readers of this insightful portrayal of Paulo Freire, his words of wisdom and also indignation concerning the nature of, not a reformist but, a revolutionary educational practice:

It is with profound conviction and, above all, in the democratic practice of this revolution that we can find great teachings for the struggle of the [oppressed] people. The popular content and the revolutionary practice of democracy understood as strategic value that can make educational practices possible and, above all, can create openness and an indispensable flexibility in the revolutionary process that begin to take shape in the answers to the concrete reality, aspirations and needs of the [oppressed] people.

It is in this context that the seemingly greater power of this Revolution can be generated: the moral and ethical power of the people who are heroically capable to confront the most criminal investments of North-American imperialism and the grave economic and social consequences that they provoke.[1]

These prophetic words not only unveil the cruelties of an obscene capitalism which we are currently witnessing, but they also emanate from a deep love for humanity that left Paulo with no other choice but to courageously denounce a world (dis)order that remains deaf to the cries of ten thousand children who die of hunger every day in the world.

NOTES

[1] Paulo Freire, *Pedagogia do Compromisso: América Latina e Educação Popular* (São Paulo, Brazil: Villa das letras Editora, 2008), pp. 64–65.

Donaldo Macedo, Professor
University of Massachusetts, Boston

ACKNOWLEDGEMENTS

A grateful acknowledgement first goes to Nita Freire, Donaldo Macedo and Peter McLaren for opening and closing our book with such passion and love, and to all our contributors for sharing their heartfelt memories about Paulo. A special thanks goes to our copy editor Patricia Harriman, College of Educational Studies. Chapman University, whose diligence, editing expertise, and consistent good humor has been invaluable in making *Memories of Paulo* a reality. Paulo was virtually unknown to her at the beginning of the project. Now, through her close readings of all the submissions, she too has "come to know" Paulo.

Second, our deep appreciation goes to Alexandre Oliveira for the translation of Nita Freire's work from Portuguese to English, also Dan Whitesell, Irvine Valley Community College, and Fernando Hernandez, University of California Irvine, for the translation from Spanish into English of the article by Ester Perez. We also thank John D. Holst and María Alicia Vetter for the translation of Rolando Pinto's entry from the Spanish.

FOREWORD

Presented in both English, and the Original Portuguese

Paulo Freire, *the eternal boy.*

Of all the stories I could tell about my husband Paulo Freire's personality, I believe one is most important to tell, to instigate and stimulate educators toward the world of imagination and of creation. And that is to have a conversation with those who *talk to* me about his *boyish* side, which he fortunately never lost.

Paulo was a *boy*, with a great and profound critical capacity, as he devoted himself, even at an adult age, "to the things that only children do and think." He would hide behind the door so I would find him. He was amused by the most ingenuous comedians possible. He would be exultant at my complimenting him on his beautiful whistling. He surrendered himself with great tenderness to his childhood heroes, chief among who was Tom Mix, with his unshakable belief—it might be cruel to say a child's belief—in people's good faith, without ever taking into account how ill-advised their behavior might be. Deep down, Paulo never wanted to lose his *childlike joy* and his great tolerance regarding human frailties.

At certain times, I thought it might be important to call his attention to those ways of his, his limitless *generosity in giving of himself* to others, in fact, one of his greatest virtues, I must recognize, but he would *pay me no mind*. He never changed in that. He remained in his *childlike stance* to the day of his death:

> Nita, it does not matter, what they do with what I say, with what I think and do. If they distort me, that is not my problem; it is the problem of whoever does that!!!

I would like, however, to take a moment in this narrative about my husband to make some considerations around what the figure of Tom Mix meant to him. I have spoken about this "hero's" image to Paulo in two of my books[1], but I believe it is important to speak here and one more time about his relationship with this character-artist.

I had previously conducted an analysis of the emotional repercussion of the North-American actor upon Paulo, but now, I would like to focus on a more epistemological approach, however, without abandoning the emotional. In other words, I now want to speak in more detail about an adult artist from Hollywood, from such distant parts, who "told a great deal about himself" to a poor, Brazilian, northeastern *boy* who did not know the fantasy world of the movies, nor the stories of "good facing evil," already so characteristic, at the beginning of the 20th century, of our brothers to the north. Those stories are the generative matrix of the culture—not always moral, but unfortunately moralistic—of the Yankees. But it was those stories of that culture that awakened in the Recifean *boy* an identification

xix

between Tom Mix's "dreams" and his own, even if those were not clearly perceived as a problem to be confronted and were, therefore, not conscious. It was a simulation of the truth to one and, to the other, the truth he could not understand to its full magnitude.

Paulo was acquainted with the elitist language of discrimination, of "do you know who you are speaking with," "this inferior race think they are people," "black men and women are only good for heavy labor," a language that caused him disgust even before he understood the reason for being of that discourse on the part of the oppressors. After all, contrary to those, he was always, since he was a boy, *with* and *in favor of* the weak, the exploited, and the oppressed. In childhood, that was so out of sensibility and intuition. In his adult life, it was out of political conviction and ethical solidarity.

Clearly, Paulo had no way of realizing the differences between reality and dream, between truly living the poverty he found himself in, experiencing every sort of need, and wanting to be a modern Robin Hood. The fact is, however, that his indignation was alive within from a tender age, and Tom Mix helped him to emotionally *see, to be*, in fact, in the same position of concern as the actor's—be that real or simulated—*in favor of* justice. That is to say, being *against the oppressors* as much as his childhood idol, who was, thus, a live presence throughout his life, from his *boyhood world of make-believe* to his death.

The American cowboy, therefore, no doubt had an important influence upon the adult Paulo's *boyish ways of being*. It was Tom Mix who led my husband to begin to understand, besides the behavior of the "good men" in the cruel northeast where he lived, what he himself felt and intuited: the perverse adult world of oppression, the meanness of the powerful, as he would later say so many times, whether in the fight against sexism, racism, and against brutal social-class conditions, or with respect to any other forms of elitist discrimination against the many "minorities" in society.

As a boy, Paulo picked up, in the cowboy's story, his stance before defenseless women, on a vein that was to be taken seriously. The defenseless female in Tom Mix reached him as a metaphor that he, *boyishly*, never let go of. In fact, Paulo enjoyed bringing up the metaphor, and did so many times, as the starting point for his political, ethical, educational argumentations. That metaphor was a starting point for the process of *conscientization*.

I am speaking of my realization that Tom Mix was a mythical presence, a necessary hero in the construction of childhood dreams, but it also remained present in my husband, in spite of all the obvious, profound, and critical overcoming, in Paulo's revolutionary and humanist utopia, mediated by *conscientization*. Watching the Tom Mix films at about ten years of age or a bit more meant the concretization of what he wanted and dreamed of for his world: understanding the reason for being and helping those with whom he interacted or whom he saw stumble along in search of nothing or nobody, through the streets of Recife. Those were a boy's dreams, yet they were dreams founded on the *life ethic* that he would come to create. Obviously, I repeat, it was not clearly laid out in his childhood dreams and conjectures, but it became concrete in his adult age. In the last ten years of his life, Paulo countless times, wherever we went, in our pilgrimage throughout the world, especially in the USA, looked for at least one Tom Mix film of the many he had seen in his childhood days.

"Nita, I would so like to see again the full-length movies starred in by my buddy Tom Mix." That sentence, repeated by Paulo so many times, gave me, since I married him, and it gives me to this day, the certainty that Tom Mix represented much more to my husband, in his childhood imagination, more than a simple movie meant to entertain adults and "*plantear*" (a word from the Spanish language that he regretted not having in Brazilian Portuguese) goodness in the souls of children. I am sure that to Paulo, Tom Mix represented much more than adventure stories about a justice-loving character in movies made for children.

In the twenties and thirties of the last century, differently from today's grotesque and hideous "Hollywoodian" adventures with their outlandish and deadly machines or gigantic and terrifying insects, which do nothing more than provide "childhood" concreteness to the meanness of these globalization times and of neoliberalism, Tom Mix films *said* something that touched the souls of those who dreamt of a better world. With his soul, his *boyish* sensibility and sweetness, Paulo realized that, I am certain of it, at a tender age.

Nowadays, films made for adolescents do not mean or are not able to realize life as a *human adventure of human greatness* in the human world, a seeking for the best for *human existence* and the realization of its ontological destiny: that of happiness and justice. Paulo's sensibility allowed him to become enchanted by such things, as was his beloved brother Themístocles, at the poor and modest Casa Forte theater in Recife.

Paulo's *critical understanding of education* was born out of his wise and profound reflection and of various sorts of theoretical reading, from the starting point of his observations and intuitions about his northeastern reality, but also out of those "small" things that he experienced, that he lived through. Paulo's *critical understanding of education* was born, as he would say himself: from his childhood, his *reading* of the life experiences that he went through, felt, and reflected upon. It was born from his most remote childhood *readings of the world*, which in his adult life gained the strength of categories for analysis and reflection. We must not doubt that those Tom Mix stories populated Paulo's creative mind, for he never forgot them or him. Tom Mix stories simply made sense to the intuition of a sad and poor child, but one already greatly sensitive to and with solidarity toward human dramas.

Back in the eighties and nineties, when Paulo insisted upon finding, in some store somewhere out there in the world, one of the Tom Mix movies, he was aware of the importance of his dreams, his childhood enchantment, and of preserving those dreams and enchantment in his adult life, as a thinker of education. Paulo's greatest dream was the utopian dream for better days, in a truly democratic society. That was a dream he dreamed since his childhood, one he brought with him throughout his life, one he deliberately never wanted to lose. On the contrary, by taking them seriously, he was able to incorporate them, build them into, his critical-utopian dreams for the transformation of societies, for a better world.

The final words in the book I wrote about my husband[2] are precisely about his boyish side, Paulo's *childlike facet*:

> I, thus, finalize this Paulo Freire biography, as painful as it was to me, as permeated by moments of extreme joy as it was, as I recalled facts, moments, feelings, and emotions and wrote about them with his words, joyful words of his, because even when speaking about his own death, he spoke from the depths of his childlike joy in having been able to "return home," in having returned to his beloved country. His joy was in his being boyishly open to LIFE. It was in the boy's pleasure at being alive. Paulo would say, about the childlike joy that oriented his entire life to the day of his death, about his whole Life history: 'Oh boy! That childlike joy is still very much alive and still childlike. I think I am going to live for a long time still and die in Brazil. Well, then, when I die, that joy will be childlike still.' (Freire, p. 621)

Having received the title of "Bambino Permanente" (Eternal Boy) from the Biblioteca Comunale de Ponsacco, Pisa, Italy, presented to him in Reggio Emilia, on March 31, 1990, demonstrates that many of those who read Paulo felt that within his rigorous words there lay the *hidden boy* that he always was.

It is true; the greatest, the most beautiful trait of this political-ethical-educational thinker who was Paulo Freire is his having had the capacity for critiquing, for powerfully denouncing the dramas of life, without losing, at any point throughout his presence in the world, his way of being a responsible adult who knew how to love and be happy, and therefore, having *announced* the new as only *boys* who are pure, serious, and adult in character can do.

Nita Freire, 2009
Translated into English by Alexandre Oliveira
Original Portuguese follows

Paulo Freire, *o eterno menino*.

De todas as histórias que eu poderia contar sobre a personalidade de Paulo Freire, meu marido, acredito que a mais importante para atrair, instigar e estimular educadores (as) para o mundo da imaginação e da criação, é conversar com quem me lê, sobre o seu *lado menino*, que, felizmente ele nunca perdeu.

Com enorme e profunda capacidade de crítica Paulo foi um *menino* ao se entregar, mesmo na idade adulta, "às coisas que só as crianças fazem e pensam". Escondia-se atrás da porta para que eu o encontrasse. Alegrava-se com os comediantes mais ingênuos possíveis. Ficava exultante com os meus elogios pelo seu belo assoviar. Entregava-se com grande ternura aos seus heróis de infância, o maior deles Tom Mix; e na sua crença inabalável ___seria cruel dizer numa crença de criança? ___ na boa fé das pessoas, sem nunca ter levado em conta o temerário no comportamento destes e destas. No fundo Paulo nunca quis perder sua *alegria-menina* e sua enorme tolerância com relação às fragilidades humanas.

Em certos momentos pensei que seria importante chamar-lhe a atenção para com esse jeito sem limites de *generosidade de entrega* aos outros e outras, aliás, devo reconhecer, uma de suas virtudes maiores, mas ele não *me dava ouvidos*. Nunca mudou nisso. Permaneceu com essa *postura-menina* até o dia de sua morte.

*Nita, não importa o que fazem com o que digo e com o que penso e faço. Se
me distorcem o problema não é meu, é de quem o faz!!!*

Gostaria, entretanto, de me deter nesta narrativa sobre o meu marido fazendo
algumas considerações em torno do que a figura de Tom Mix representou para ele.
Falei sobre a imagem deste "herói" para Paulo em dois de meus livros mas creio
que é muito importante falar aqui e outra vez sobre a sua relação com este artista-
personagem.

Antes eu tinha feito uma análise sobre a repercussão emocional do ator norte-
americano sobre Paulo, agora quero focar-me numa abordagem mais epistemológica,
sem entretanto, abandonar a emocional. Em outras palavras, agora quero falar mais
detalhadamente sobre um adulto artista de Hollywood, de plagas tão distantes, que
"contou muito de si" a um *menino* pobre, brasileiro, nordestino, que nem conhecia
o mundo da fantasia do cinema e nem as histórias "do bem enfrentando o mal", tão
próprias, já no início do século XX, dos nossos irmãos do Norte. Histórias que são
a matriz geradora da cultura – nem sempre moral, mas infelizmente moralista – dos
yankes. Mas, foram as histórias dessa cultura que despertaram no *menino* recifense
identificar os "sonhos" de Tom Mix com os seus, mesmo que ainda não percebidos
claramente como um problema a ser enfrentado e portanto, não conscientes. Era
para um a simulação da verdade e para o outro uma verdade que não conseguia
entender na sua magnitude.

Paulo conhecia a linguagem elitista e discriminatória do "sabe com quem está
falando?", "essa raça inferior pensa que é gente!", "negros e negras só servem
mesmo para o trabalho pesado", que lhe causava ojeriza mesmo antes de compreender
a razão de ser deste discurso dos opressores. Porque, ao contrário, desde menino
ele esteve sempre *com* e *em favor* dos fracos e dos explorados (as) e oprimidos (as).
Na sua infância, por sensibilidade e intuição. Na sua vida adulta, por convicção
política e solidariedade ética.

É claro que Paulo não tinha condições de perceber as diferenças entre a realidade
e o sonho, entre viver de verdade a pobreza nela metida e nela sofrendo toda sorte
de necessidades e querer ser um Robin Hood moderno. Mas, o fato é que, sua
indignação, estava viva nele desde tenra idade e Tom Mix ajudou-o a *ver*
emocionalmente, *estar,* de fato, na mesma posição de preocupação do ator –
verdadeira ou simulada –, *em favor* da justiça. O que vale dizer, estar *contra os
opressores (as)* tanto quanto o seu ídolo de infância, que, assim, foi uma presença
viva por toda a sua vida desde seu *mundo do faz de conta de menino* até a sua morte.

O cow-boy norte-americano, portanto, teve sem dúvida alguma, uma influência
importante, no *modo de ser do menino* Paulo adulto. Foi Tom Mix que induziu
meu marido a começar a entender, ao lado do comportamento dos "homens de
bem" do nordeste cruel onde vivia, o que sentia e intuía: o perverso mundo adulto
da opressão, a malvadez dos poderosos, como dirá depois tantas vezes. Quer na
defesa contra o machismo, o racismo e a situação de classe social brutais, quer com
relação a quaisquer outras formas de discriminação elitista e discriminatória contra
outras tantas "minorias" da sociedade.

Paulo, quando menino, captou na história do cow-boy, na postura deste diante
das mulheres indefesas um veio a ser levado a sério. A mulher indefesa de Tom

Mix chegou a ele como uma metáfora, que *meninamente* nunca abandonou. Aliás, Paulo gostava e trouxe, muitas vezes, a metáfora como um ponto de partida para as suas argumentações políticas, éticas e educativas. A metáfora, como ponto de partida para o processo de **conscientização**.

Estou dizendo de minha constatação de que Tom Mix foi uma presença mítica, do herói necessário à construção dos sonhos da infância, mas também, permaneceu presente, em meu marido, com toda a superação óbvia, profunda e crítica, na utopia revolucionária e humanista de Paulo, intermediada pela **conscientização**.

Assistir às películas de Tom Mix aos 10 anos ou pouco mais de idade representava a concretização do que ele queria e sonhava para o seu mundo: entender a razão de ser e ajudar as pessoas com as quais se relacionava ou via tropegamente caminhar à procura de nada e de ninguém, pelas ruas do Recife. Eram sonhos de menino, entretanto sonhos fundamentados na *ética da vida*, que viria a criar. Obviamente, repito, não claramente posta nas suas conjecturas e sonhos infantis, mas concretizadas na sua idade adulta.

Nos 10 últimos anos de sua vida Paulo procurou inúmeras vezes, por todo canto aonde andávamos, na nossa andarilhagem pelo mundo, sobretudo nos USA, por um filme sequer de Tom Mix dos tantos que tinha assistido nos seus tempos de infância.

Nita, queria tanto ver novamente "os filmes de longa-metragem protagonizado por meu camarada Tom Mix",

Esta sua frase, repetida por Paulo tantas vezes, me dava, desde que me casei com ele e continua até hoje me dando, uma certeza de que, para meu marido, Tom Mix representou no seu imaginário infantil muito mais do que uma simples película para distrair os adultos e "*plantear*" (palavra da língua espanhola que ele lamentava não existir na brasileira) bondade nas almas infantis. Tenho certeza de que para Paulo Tom Mix representava muito mais do que histórias de aventura de personagem amante da justiça de filmes destinados às crianças.

Nos anos 20 e 30 do século passado, diferentemente das aventuras grotescas e horripilantes das holywoodianas atuais com suas máquinas mirabolantes e mortíferas ou insetos gigantescos e apavorantes, que nada mais fazem do que dar concretude "infantil" à malvadez dos tempos da globalização e do neoliberalismo, as películas de Tom Mix *diziam* alguma coisa que tocava a alma dos que sonhavam com um mundo melhor. Paulo com sua alma, sensibilidade e doçura *meninas* constatou isto, estou certa disso, em tenra idade.

Atualmente as películas feitas para os adolescentes não querem ou não podem perceber a vida como uma *aventura humana da grandeza humana* no mundo do humano procurando o melhor para a *existência humana* realizar o seu destino ontológica: o da felicidade e o da justiça. Coisas, que a sensibilidade de Paulo se deixava encantar e ao seu muito querido irmão Themístocles, no pobre e modesto cinema de Casa Forte, do Recife.

A *compreensão crítica de educação* de Paulo nasceu de suas reflexões sábias e profundas e de leituras teóricas diversas, a partir de suas observações e intuições sobre a realidade nordestina, mas também dessas "pequenas" coisas que ele viveu, que ele experimentou. A *compreensão crítica de educação* de Paulo nasceu, como ele mesmo dizia: na sua infância, na *leitura* de suas experiências de vida vividas, sentidas e refletidas. Nas suas *leituras de mundo* da infância mais remota, que na sua vida adulta tomou força de categorias de análise e reflexão. Não podemos duvidar de que as histórias de Tom Mix povoaram a criativa mente de Paulo, pois daquelas e deste ele jamais esqueceu. É que as histórias de Tom Mix fizeram sentido nele pela intuição de criança pobre e triste, mas já muito sensível e solidário aos dramas humanos.

Quando nos anos 80 e 90 Paulo insistia em encontrar em alguma loja de vídeos espalhada por este mundo um dos filmes de Tom Mix ele sabia da importância de seus sonhos, de seus encantamentos de infância e da preservação desses sonhos e desse encantamento na vida adulta, de pensador da educação. O sonho maior de Paulo era o sonho utópico de dias melhores, numa sociedade realmente democrática. Sonho que sonhou desde sua infância e, que carregou por toda a sua vida, o qual deliberadamente jamais quis perder. Ao contrário, os levando a sério os pode incorporar e embutir nos seus sonhos crítico-utópico de transformação das sociedades, de um mundo melhor.

As últimas palavras do livro que escrevi sobre o meu marido são justamente sobre o lado menino, a *face-menina* de Paulo."Finalizo, assim, esta biografia de Paulo Freire, tão dolorosa que foi para mim, permeada de momentos de extrema alegria, ao relembrar fatos, momentos, sentimentos e emoções e escrever sobre eles, com palavras dele, alegres palavras dele, porque mesmo falando de sua própria morte ele falava do mais fundo da sua alegria-menina de ter podido "voltar para casa", de ter voltado ao seu querido país. De meninamente estar aberto à VIDA. De com gosto menino estar vivo.

Paulo falava da alegria menina que norteou toda a sua vida até o dia de sua morte, de toda a sua *história de Vida*: Puxa rapaz! A alegria menina continua vivíssima e menina ainda. Acho que ainda vou viver muito e morrer no Brasil. Pois bem, quando eu morrer, esta alegria ainda estará menina!" (Freire: 621)

Ter recebido o título de "Bambino Permanente" (Eterno Menino") da Biblioteca Comunale de Ponsacco, Pisa, Itália, a ele entregue em Reggio Emilia, em 31 de março de 1990, demonstra que muitos dos que leram a Paulo sentiam que em sua rigorosas palavras estava *escondido o menino* que sempre foi.

É verdade, o traço maior e mais bonito deste pensador político-ético-educador que foi Paulo Freire foi ter tido a capacidade de criticar contundentemente denunciando os dramas da vida, sem contudo ter perdido, em nenhum momento de sua presença no mundo, a sua maneira de ter sido um adulto responsável que soube amar e ser feliz, e por isso ter *anunciado* um novo, que só *meninos* de caráter puro, sério, de adulto, podem fazer.

NOTES

[1] Nita e Paulo: crônicas de amor. Olho d´água, *Nita e Paulo* crônicas de amor, Preface by Marta Suplicy, São Paulo: Olho D'Água, 1998; *Chronicles of love: my life with Paulo Freire.* Preface by Marta Suplicy, Introdution by Donaldo Macedo. New York; Washington, DC; Baltimore; Bern; Frankfurt Main; Berlin; Brussels; Vienna; Oxford: Lang, 2001; and *Paulo Freire: uma história de*

vida. Preface by Alípio Casali and Vera Barreto. Indaiatuba: Editora Villa das Letras, 2006. Jabuti Award 2007, "The Best biography book", Second Place. Not yet translated to English.

[2] e *Paulo Freire: uma história de vida*. Indaiatuba: Editora Villa das Letras, 2006, p. 621.

Nita Freire

Dr. Ana Maria (Nita) Araújo Freire is an international speaker and author of many books and articles, including: Paulo Freire: uma história de vida (2006) and Chronicles of Love: My Life with Paulo Freire (2001).

INTRODUCTION

For remembering, as we have conceived it, essentially implies consciousness of itself.

Aristotle, 350 BCE

What are memories? They are the indelible impressions we have of lived experiences. They mark moments when we have grown in our development; the time when a new child was born, a loved one has died; when our eyes have been opened to a new way of viewing the world; of understanding life in all of its complexities.

In this fast paced, technological world where *memory* is often viewed as how much information a computer chip can store without regard to its content, or how many gigabytes or megabytes a computer has, we reflect on the origin and meaning of the word *memory*–in the spirit of Paulo Freire (who always sought the meaning of words)–and seek to rekindle its more historical humane relevance. Drawing from the Sanskrit roots smar *to remember* through Indo-European smer *memory*, the ancient Greek mermeros/*care laden* and the Latin *mermera* with its connotation of both *memory* and *mindfulness*, this collection is not necessarily a concern for how much or how many memories we have of Paulo Freire but rather is an account of the care-laden and mindful intensity submerged within them.

With this in mind, our authors were asked to contribute their memories of Paulo with memories understood as "both to the power of remembering and to what is remembered."[1] The initial call for contributions read:

> We are writing to invite you to join us in a book project dedicated to the memory of Paulo Freire. As you know, Paulo will have been gone from us ten years come 2007. To mark this occasion, we would like to get together with those of us to whom he has meant so much as a friend, a mentor, and a model and put together a book of remembrances. The emphasis of the book is going to be on the human side of which he shared so much with us. We like to include stories of personal nature that tell what kind of human being he was, with his joys and sadness, strengths and weaknesses, courage, humility, and sense of humor, particularly when the joke was on him. We believe Paulo embodied his teachings in his being, and this is what we are trying to capture. This is not going to be a book that illustrates his pedagogy, or explicates it. We prefer that these essays be short, about 1,000 words.

A follow-up call for submissions clarified two limitations: It requested first, contributions from those who had had personal contact with Paulo in one way or another, and second, to place emphases not on his theory or pedagogy per se but rather upon who he was and remains as an individual. However as we progressed in the book's development, it became clear that, while most of the respondents adhered to our stated limitations, *a few* demurred. Some of the contributors wrote about Paulo as they got to know him through his work. They insisted they knew him quite well in spite of never having the chance to meet him. A few others who did know him, personally, seemed not to be able separate him from his theory in that who he was could not be parsed from what he thought. Others thought that either 1,000 words were not necessary or on the other hand, insufficient. In fact, the average number of words turned out to be around 1500. After asking ourselves what would Paulo likely do, we accepted these entries; the quality of their submissions clearly trumped our stated limitations.

Thus, we have worked for several years putting together this tribute for Paulo, whom we consider to be the most significant educational philosopher and practitioner of the second half of the twentieth century. We embarked on this journey by gathering the memories of people who knew Paulo as a way to honor him after the 10th anniversary of his death. Contributions came from writers throughout the United States and other parts of the world. All of these "students" and friends of Paulo cherish the moments they shared with him. They represent a wide range of individuals who knew him at different periods of his life and in different situations from onetime encounters to relationships spanning over thirty years. For the most part, these individuals continue to practice as critical pedagogues in diverse fields and localities with a common commitment to social justice and transformative education, all in the spirit of Paulo's legacy.

To reiterate a bit, we wished to commemorate him with stories about his personal side, a social dimension of his person that those who read his books and/or other writings rarely got to sense. In this manner, we meant to reveal his many facets as a deeply humane individual who impacted the lives of many, from a colleague who worked with him in Chile in 1968 to a ten-year-old child who attended Disneyland with him in the mid 1980s.

In our attempt to show the intricacies of hope and love in this man, we called on the colleagues and friends who had come to know Paulo Freire, the man. It could be that they spoke with him at an invited event, or that they worked closely by his side on an educational initiative; they might have shared a meal with him on one of his many international visits, or sat with him to engage in dialogue; or they might have merely attended one of his presentations. All of these writers give their accounts of those special moments where they came to know Paulo in all his naked humanness.

We hope that readers of our collection of stories will find the format simple and unpretentious. Paulo often was apt to declare the right of individuals to speak in their own voice as a moral necessity. To honor this claim, we have kept editing to a minimum as much as possible. We know that is how Paulo would have liked it.

We invited Paulo's beloved wife and inspiration, Nita Freire and his dear friend, translator, and comrade, Donaldo Macedo to set the stage by writing the Foreword and Preface, respectively, with his colleague, Peter McLaren constructing the Afterword. Not surprisingly, we three editors also have taken the opportunity to share our experiences with Paulo and the memories of how he touched our lives. We organized the book somewhat chronologically, around different periods, beginning with the 1960s and 70s, then into the very busy 1980s and ending in the 1990s. While these are not exact, we drew from the writings to get an idea of the approximate timeline. We thank our many contributors for their willingness to reflect the moments they shared with Paulo Freire and that they hold so dear. It is indeed a tribute to Paulo that after so many years the memories remain so vivid and full of love. For it is out of love that Paulo did his work and lived his life.

Finally, it is out of commitment that we continue our work and live our lives in service of a better world where oppression is no longer acceptable and freedom is the result of a libratory pedagogy for young and old, poor and affluent, privileged professional and worker alike. We seek the life of Paulo to serve as a reminder that with hope, all is possible in our quest for a more just world. Thank you, Paulo. We continue to miss you and will always remember you.

Introduction by Editors: Tom Wilson, Peter Park and Anaida Colon-Muñiz

NOTES

[1] memory. (2009). In *Merriam-Webster Online Dictionary*. Retrieved July 7, 2009, from http://www. merriam-webster.com/dictionary/memory

FROM THE 1960s

Cynthia Brown

Alma Flor Ada

John Pinto Contreras

John McFadden

CYNTHIA BROWN

1. REMEMBERING PAULO FREIRE

As the young wife (27 years old) of a Peace Corps doctor arriving in Recife, on the northeast coast of Brazil, in July of 1965, forty-two years ago, I knew no word of Portuguese and keeping my nine-month-old son alive and healthy seemed my most urgent task.

Recife was then a city of a million people, seventy percent of whom could not read or write. Paulo Freire, a native of the city, was not among the residents; he had fled first to Bolivia, then to Santiago, Chile, ten months earlier. A military coup had taken control of Brazilian national and state governments in April 1964, and Freire had been under house arrest for several months, then jailed for seventy days, before he left the country for what turned out to be sixteen years of exile.

Freire came to be seen as a dangerous man by the military authorities because he believed that the university should be a base for the education of all Brazilians, not just the elite. While teaching philosophy and education at the university, Freire also coordinated the Adult Education Program of the Popular Culture Movement. In February 1962 he became the director of the university's newly established cultural Extension Service; there he developed his literacy program, supported by the U.S. Agency for International Development (USAID) with enough funds to run a pilot project and train seventy coordinators.

Fewer than two years later, USAID terminated its assistance; it feared the rise of communism among the former illiterates. A coalition of Socialist, Labor, and Communist parties had elected the mayor of Recife, Miguel Arraes, to the governorship of the state of Pernambuco in October 1962. Two farm worker strikes occurred in 1963, the second one involving 25% of the state's farm workers. The upper classes became frightened by the growing political awareness of the masses and retaliated with the military coup of April 1964.

I learned of Freire's work from the university student who exchanged language lessons with me. She had worked with Freire's "circles of culture," and as she told me how they functioned, I realized their significance and wanted to learn more. Visiting the office of USAID, I posed as a researcher documenting how communistic Recife had been before the military takeover. Only under this ruse were they willing to give me copies of the slides that Freire used to provoke discussions and copies of the primers written by two of his colleagues, who could not stick to Freire's decision that the generation of the words and the initial sentences should occur as a process by the learners and the coordinators working together.

T. Wilson, P. Park and A. Colón-Muñiz (eds.), Memories of Paulo, 3–5.
© *2010 Sense Publishers. All Rights Reserved.*

I returned to the states in 1967, and three years later Freire's major book, *The Pedagogy of the Oppressed*, was published in English. I loved the philosophical language that he so masterfully invented—but why didn't he just tell people in plain words what he had done in Recife? I thought his readers would need more than inspiration, something specific to go on.

A few years later Herb Kohl and I organized a teacher education program in Berkeley to prepare people of diverse backgrounds for elementary school teaching. I began telling our students the details of Paulo's literacy program, and Herb led the discussions of how these ideas might be applied to Berkeley's classrooms. In 1978 my essay describing how Freire's circles of culture operated was published by the Alternative Schools Network as *Literacy in Thirty Hours*, together with two interviews with teachers who discussed how to apply Freire's ideas to teaching children.

Eventually, Paulo and Elza visited Berkeley. I was invited to Jack London's home to meet them, along with a large group of Freire's admirers. During the eager discussions that ensued, I posed to Paulo the question that I couldn't shake; why hadn't he been more specific in his writings about his teaching methods in Recife?

Paulo laughed and replied something like this: he knew the tendency of people to copy the methods of other teachers; that was exactly what he believed did not work to empower the learners or the teachers. To avoid being copied, he simply withheld any details that could be copied and focused instead on describing the conceptions that underlay his work.

How right he was! But Paulo didn't scold me for trying to lay out the steps of his dialogue in the circles of culture; I can only hope that my account has not done too much damage of the sort he feared.

After dinner, as we gathered in the front hall to leave, the other women and I had a surprise that engraved itself on my memory. Elza fetched Paulo's jacket out of the closet and helped him into it; the great revolutionary couldn't put on his own jacket! I don't recall that we said anything to him about this at the time, and I remember Paulo later joking about how much he had to learn about women's liberation.

After Paulo returned to Brazil in 1980 to teach at the University of São Paulo, his friend there, Moacir Gadotti, posed to Paulo the same questions that one of Karl Marx's daughters had put to Marx, so that the answers could be compared. At Freire's death, a Brazilian newspaper published both sets of answers; here are a few of Paulo's answers, with Marx's in parenthesis:

Your most characteristic trait:	tolerance (coherence of purpose)
Your idea of happiness:	struggle (struggle)
Your idea of disgrace:	oppression (submission)
The defect you are most guilty of:	mistaken love (incredulity)
Your greatest dislike:	intellectual arrogance (Martin Tupper)
Your preferred activity:	teaching and learning (browsing second-hand bookstores)

It seems fitting that Brazil should have produced such a man as Paulo Freire. His tolerance, good humor, flexibility and absolute trust in the people seem as Brazilian as bossa nova, taken to the nth degree.

Cynthia Stokes Brown, Professor Emerita
Dominican University of California

ALMA FLOR ADA

2. PAULO FREIRE ALWAYS PRESENT

Paulo Freire became a part of my life, as it has happened for many, through his written words. As a university student in Lima, Perú in the early sixties, I read his essays smuggled from Chile in mimeographed copies. In the early seventies I rejoiced seeing that his thoughts had been incorporated into the Peruvian Educational Reform conceived and directed by the philosopher Augusto Salazar Bondy, who so lucidly had written about theories of domination. While this Reform was never fully carried on, partially due to Salazar Bondy's premature death, and mainly because in Perú any form of social justice continues to be the need of many and the dream of a few, the documents developed to support it continue to be some of the best conceptualizations of national popular education.

My first personal encounter with Freire was in Sacramento, California, at a small gathering in a private home. He was already sitting, ready to speak, when I got there with my daughter Rosalma, and sat on the floor next to him. When he finished speaking his first words to me were very direct: "And, who are you?" I simply answered: "We had a common dear friend..." At the mention of Augusto Salazar, a bond was established that would only grow as time went on.

Thanks to Martin Carnoy's efforts to bring Freire to Stanford, I was able to participate in an intensive course with Paulo. As a Latin American woman, a mother, living far from my country, it was natural to spend time with Paulo's wife Elza, who was with him in that trip. Her comforting and nurturing presence had a great impact on me.

Paulo returned alone to California a few times more, and on a couple of occasions stayed at my home. And if Elza was not physically with him, she was always present in his conversation.

Of course, Paulo's words and teachings were a constant in my life. Early on, when my daughter was a high school student, she had challenged me: "I like to listen to your presentations, I wish my teachers would treat me like you treat your students, and I have even read *The Pedagogy of the Oppressed*... but why doesn't it feel to me that at home you are doing what you are teaching? It seems at home there is only one voice–yours!" This moment was one of the deciding moments in my life, which forced me to rethink my whole relationship with my children... and I have Paulo to thank for the firm commitment to walk the talk, to embody and become at every moment what I taught. And my life has been so much more meaningful for it.

Most of the dissertations I chaired at the University of San Francisco incorporated Paulo's teachings on Critical Pedagogy and Participatory Research, and as my students taught me what they had learned from Freire, I continued learning

T. Wilson, P. Park and A. Colón-Muñiz (eds.), Memories of Paulo, 7–8.

from him as well. And he became one of the binding forces of the family the students were creating through their solidarity and their commitment to justice, inclusion and peace.

During one of his visits to speak at University of San Francisco, the Dean at the time and I took Paulo to lunch. I knew Paulo as someone who could truly enjoy a good meal. Unfortunately, this Peruvian restaurant served very large portions on oversize dishes. When Paulo saw the serving in front of him, he became very pensive, with eyes filled with tears he said: "In my country, a whole family could eat from a dish like this…" He never touched his food, and neither did we. For many years the Dean would say to me: "Remember the look on Freire's face?" As with any of us, there were many layers to Paulo Freire, but compassion was always there at the core, and on occasion it could overtake him.

Elza's death had a devastating effect on Paulo. And in subsequent encounters he wanted to share and discuss his loss with someone who had treasured Elza's friendship, someone who also knew about losses and about cherished presences that survive death. And I was glad to be there for him as he had been there always for me.

Everyone who cared for Paulo rejoiced when he found a new strength in the relationship with Nita, who became his second wife. In São Paolo, I had several conversations with Paulo and Nita, about what this second beginning meant for both of them–at a park, walking through an artisan's fair, visiting Elza's tomb, and repeatedly at their home which Nita had redecorated very beautifully, with her collections of Brazilian art. These conversations stand out in my memory as a proof of their authentic and responsible way of encountering daily life. They were able to incorporate their love for their previous spouses and children into their own new-found love in a very truthful way, while at the same time preserving the glory they have discovered in their feelings for each other.

I remember Paulo jokingly saying one afternoon that he enjoyed "futbol" (soccer) because it was the only moment he could really just watch and not reflect about what was going on… but then he burst out laughing saying: "But, who wants to be dead, anyway?" Reflection, as well as love, was not only a way of life for Paulo Freire; it was life itself.

Alma Flor Ada, Professor Emerita
University of San Francisco

ROLANDO PINTO CONTRERAS[1]

3. ON THE REALITY OF THEORETICAL LANGUAGE

A Particular Reflective Experience with Paulo Freire

With this article I want to give an account of a situation in which I participated with Paulo Freire at a crucial point in October of 1968, at the commencement of a series of courses for peasant leaders—beneficiaries of the process of Agrarian Reform that was taking place in Chile (1967–1973)–organized by the Department of Peasant Training, Corporation for Agrarian Reform (CORA), Ministry of Agriculture. The professional coordinators wanted Paulo Freire's participation in these courses, but they were concerned about the phenomenological language that, in those days, dominated all of Paulo's discourse and thinking. The coordinators asked if someone from his team of Chileans would translate into "popular rural language" his theoretical and conceptual ideas. What I think *is* remarkable, and which made an indelible mark on me as an educator, was the reflection that Paulo Freire made of this demand in the presence of the very functionaries that made this request, as well as before some of us members of the ICIRA training team that, until his departure for the U.S., constituted his work team and institutional support[2].

First, and with the ease and concern that were so characteristic of him, he began his reflections with a phenomenological reference to language in human action: it had to do with the presence of the word in lived action. In other words, language is the action with which I declare my praxis, which is nothing else but "simultaneous reflection/action." Therefore, the language that he used was not an invention or an adaptation, nor an appropriation of the word/world of the other, but the expression of the reflective/active unfolding which was indissociable from Freire himself, the making of Freire in dialogue with the oppressed of his people, and now with the Chilean peasant sectors.

Later, he continued pointing out the "inviability" of someone other than himself being able to "translate" his language without, at the same time, negating his very "reflective/active" unfolding, and thereby negating his own word/world. Such a possibility was simply an incredible manipulation: to translate Freire, negating him and causing "the translator" to negate himself or herself.

To him, this entailed a lack of recognition, of visibility and of respect toward the peasant participant himself as it presupposed that the latter had no word/world since it was considered necessary to "loan him the translated word/world" of Paulo Freire; under such circumstances, Paulo could not participate in so dehumanizing an enterprise. In its totality, this was an action conceived and undertaken as an action of negation of all those who would participate in it and, therefore, he could not be an accomplice to such a "genocide."

T. Wilson, P. Park and A. Colón-Muñiz (eds.), Memories of Paulo, 9–13.

The relation of Freire's language with peasant language has to do with a dialogue between visions of the world in which "my word, full of phenomeno-logical meanings, since this is my real word/world, is understood by the peasants when they discover in their own formulation of their own word/world their cultural and social historicity in language"[3]. Therefore, the idea is not to translate Freire but to initiate a formative action based in an interactive dialogue between a teacher/ student and various teacher/students.

But Freire did not end his reflection here; instead he turned it toward two other themes that are present in all of his subsequent work. First, his expressed desire that those who work with him not repeat him, since by doing so, they kill themselves as subjects in their construction as legitimate word/worlds, and of course they caricature Freire by making him into a static discourse. Along these lines, Freire's admonition toward his eventual collaborators was always: "reflect upon your practice, since from this should the theory that illuminates your transformation emerge."[4]

The other theme is this sort of "ontology of language"[5] that has always been present in Freirean analysis and discourse: theory without practice is mere speculation and practice without theory is pure activism. Both "speculation" and "activism" are distortions of the human meaning of educational practice.

Well then, after this profound analysis, Freire concluded by saying:

> Please, my dear friends of CORA, do not worry about translating me so that the oppressed will understand me; they recognize themselves in what I say because what I say (in a language so difficult for you), is what they live. Rather, concern yourselves with writing down your own reflections on your practice of liberation of the oppressed. That will make you much happier than to translate the discourse of this complicated Brazilian educator[6]

I sincerely believe that this almost autobiographical experience that I reclaim from my own learning with Paulo is the best homage I can offer him after the tenth anniversary of his death.

NOTES

[1] The author is Chilean. He worked with Paulo Freire in ICIRA during the years 1968 to 1970 and continued collaborating and dialoguing with him until very near the date of his lamentable death.

[2] We were part of the Training Department of ICIRA and we also were members of "Paulo Freire's team". Those who I remember as most involved were: José Luis Fiori, Marcela Gajardo, Jorge Mellado, José Nagel, and Sergio Villegas

[3] This quote documents the conversation/reflection that Freire postulated at the time, and that later on, when he began to write his book *The Pedagogy of the Oppressed*, I brought back to him in one of the many meetings we had on the team to discuss the production and the productive action of Freire's written discourse. Field notes of Rolando Pinto "Our Work with Paulo Freire in Chile: A Contribution to Popular Education"; unpublished manuscript in process.

[4] Field notes of Rolando Pinto.

[5] I take this accurate conceptualization of the reality of being contained in the action of the word, from Rafael Echeverría (1994)

[6] Field notes of Rolando Pinto.

REFERENCE

Echeverría, R. (1994). *Ontología del lenguaje* [The ontology of language]. Santiago de Chile: Dolmen Ediciones.

Rolando Pinto Contreras
School of Education, Pontifical Catholic University of Chile

Translated into English by John D. Holst and María Alicia Vetter
Original Spanish follows

ROLANDO PINTO CONTRERAS

ACERCA DE LA REALIDAD DEL LENGUAJE TEÓRICO

Una experiencia reflexiva particular con Paulo Freire

Quiero testimoniar con este artículo una situación en que me tocó participar con él en un momento crucial del inicio de los Cursos para dirigentes campesinos, beneficiarios del proceso de Reforma Agraria que se realizaba en Chile (1967/1973), en el mes de Octubre de 1968 y que eran organizados por el Departamento de Capacitación Campesina, Corporación de Reforma Agraria/CORA, Ministerio de Agricultura. Era del interés de los profesionales coordinadores de estos cursos que participara P. Freire, pero su preocupación era el lenguaje fenomenológico que en ese momento "ocupaba" todo el discurso y la reflexión de Paulo y ellos le solicitaban que alguien de su equipo de "chilenos" pudiese traducir a "lenguaje popular rural" sus propuestas "teórico-conceptuales." Lo que me parece notable y que me quedó marcado en mi formación de educador, fue la reflexión que sobre esta demanda realizó Paulo Freire, en presencia de los funcionarios que lo solicitaban y de algunos miembros del equipo de capacitación de ICIRA y que constituíamos, hasta su partida a USA, su equipo de trabajo y de apoyo institucional.

1) En primer lugar y con la tranquilidad y bondad que lo caracterizaba, inicia su reflexión con una referencia fenomenológica del lenguaje en la acción humana: se trata de una presentificación de la palabra en la acción vivida. Es decir, el lenguaje es la acción en la cual testimonio mi praxis, que no es otra cosa que "reflexión/acción a la vez." Por tanto el lenguaje que usaba él no era una invención ni una adopción ni una apropiación del mundo/palabra del otro, sino que la expresión del devenir reflexivo/activo indisociable de Freire mismo, haciendose Freire en diálogo con los oprimidos de su pueblo y ahora con los sectores campesinos chilenos.

2) Luego siguió señalando lo "inviable" que le resultaba que alguien que no fuera él pudiese "traducir" su lenguaje sin al mismo tiempo negar su propio devenir "reflexivo/activo" y por tanto, negando su propia palabra/mundo. Tal posibilidad era simplemente una manipulación increíble de traducir a Freire, negándolo y haciendo que el "traductor" se negara en su acción asimismo.

3) Que a él le parecía una falta de reconocimiento, de visibilidad y de respeto hacia el propio participante campesino ya que se suponía que éste no tenía palabra/ mundo y se le quería "prestar una palabra/mundo traducida" de Paulo Freire; y en tal circunstancia, él no podría participar en tan deshumanizante empresa. Tal empresa en su totalidad era una acción pensada y actualizada como negación de

todos los que participarían de ella y por tanto él no podría ser cómplice de tal "genocidio."

4) La relación del lenguaje Freire con lenguaje campesino, tiene que ver con un diálogo entre visiones de mundo en que "la palabra mía, impregnada de significados fenomenológicos, ya que esa es mi palabra/mundo actual, se hace comprensible para el campesino cuando este descubre en su propia formulación de su palabra/mundo su historicidad cultural y social en el lenguaje." Por tanto el tema no es traducir a Freire sino que instalar una acción formativa que se fecunde en el diálogo entre un educador/educando y varios educandos/educadores en interacción.

5) Pero Freire no termina aquí su reflexión sino que deriva la misma hacia dos otras temáticas que son constantes en toda su obra posterior: por un lado, su solicitud expresa que por favor los que trabajen con él no repitan a Freire, ya que de esa manera se matan asimismos como sujetos de su construcción como palabra/mundo legitimados y por su puesto, caricaturizan a Freire al hacerlo un discurso estático. En este sentido el aguijón formativo de Freire hacia sus eventuales colaboradores era siempre: "reflexionen su práctica, ya que de ella debiera surgir la teoría que ilumine su transformación."

6) El otro tema, es esta especie de "ontología del lenguaje" que siempre ha estado en la reflexión y el discurso freiriano: la teoría sin práctica, es una mera especulación y una práctica sin teoría es puro activismo. Siendo la "especulación" y el "activismo" dos manifestaciones distorcionantes del sentido humano de la acción educativa.

Pues bien, después de esta profunda reflexión, el propio Freire concluía:

Por favor, queridos amigos de la CORA, no se preocupen por traducirme para que me entiendan los oprimidos, ellos se reconocen en mi habla porque lo que digo (en un lenguaje tan difícil para ustedes) es lo que ellos viven, ocúpense más bien en escribir sus propias reflexiones sobre sus prácticas de liberación de los oprimidos. Eso los hará mucho más felices que traducir el discurso de este enredado educador brasilero.

Sinceramente creo que esta experiencia casi autobiográfica que rescato de mi propio aprendizaje con Paulo, es el mejor homenaje que puedo brindarle en este décimo aniversario de su muerte.

13

JOHN MCFADDEN

4. PAULO FREIRE MEMORIES

More than Ten Years after his Passing

A family trip to Chile made it possible for me to meet Paulo Freire. In Santiago, on December 28, 1968 I met Paulo Freire for the first time. An old friend had discovered Paulo's address but not the phone number, so I dropped in.

Who did I think I was about to meet? I had an idea because in 1964 I had the good fortune of having studied at Ivan Illich's *Centro de Investigaciones Culturales* in Cuernavaca. Illich himself gave several lectures on Paulo Freire's popular literacy work in Brazil. What Paulo was doing remained in my mind as something exciting, practical and oriented toward increasing the power of oppressed people to take action against the economic and social injustices visited upon them. Thus, my first memory of Paulo was hearing about his work and finding it personally inspiring, hopeful and connected to reality in such a way that I could imagine actually carrying out those ideas.

By the time I was standing in Freire's doorway in 1968, I thought he was someone who was moving ahead with a real world education/social change project while developing a theory of education and of praxis, and that I could learn from both. I had entered graduate school the year before, and was looking for a way to organize my studies so that they would emphasize social change theory and practice and help me think through what I was going to do with my own life given the values I had. What does a person with a certain set of values and ideals do in life so that work and values are congruent? Paulo turned out to be the ideal mentor for that topic and a lot more.

In the meantime, I was standing at Paulo's door and blurted out a request to study with him if by some miracle the time and place could be arranged. He said "yes." Shortly thereafter I found that Paulo would be leaving Chile and had accepted an offer to teach in a university.

In the summer of 1969 I found out that Paulo was giving a lecture series at the same Ivan Illich's institute in Cuernavaca which by that time had become known as CIDOC, *Centro de Investigactiones y Documentacion.* "This might be my chance to find the time and the place to study with him," I thought. I was working that summer with Teacher Corps on the border in the town of Tecate, Mexico. I could not be away from the job for more than a weekend, so I soon found myself on an Aeronaves de Mexico flight from Tijuana to Mexico City with a return ticket for the next day. After a bus ride to Cuernavaca and finding CIDOC, I found that Freire was really there and talked to him early the next day. A short conversation

T. Wilson, P. Park and A. Colón-Muñiz (eds.), Memories of Paulo, 15–18.
© 2010 Sense Publishers. All Rights Reserved.

on the grass outside his lecture hall, led to a "yes" from Paulo. I would be able to study with him for four weeks in August before he started teaching. His generous "yes," however, came in the midst of a linguistically tangled communication. As I tried pinning down exact time and place to start, Paulo kept referring to the fact he would be teaching in Cambridge. My heart sank. "I can't go to England," I noted. Somehow I had understood him to be talking about a university in the U.K, instead of a city in the U.S. Of course, he was really headed for Harvard which is in Cambridge, Massachusetts. I stumbled around in the conversation until finally I got his meaning and thought, "what a risk-taking man he is, to take on a tutorial with a student who mixes up such basic items as this."

His only "condition" was that I be willing to read various texts and then be prepared during the tutorial hour to ask him questions which had arisen for me. I eagerly said "yes," and thought "*dialogo*. It looks like this is going to be an experience of the 'dialogue method.'" The tutorial turned out to be one hour in the afternoon, five days a week for four weeks. It ended the weekend before he started teaching his Harvard classes. These twenty meetings were the richest education experience of my life. Example: at the first meeting Paulo handed me *On Practice* and *On Contradiction* by Mao Tse-tung. I had read a little of this and a little of that by Marx, but now found myself discussing "practice" and "contradiction" with Paulo who was a master of the concepts. They are key elements of Marx's philosophy and also key concepts utilized by Freire in his own synthesis of thought and action with regard to education. It was thrilling and it was deep, but mostly it was Paulo acting as the good dialogical teacher who was helping me clarify and think through the key concepts of "practice" and "contradiction." This was an educational revolution for me personally because previous to this experience, I had spent years being a recipient of "banking education" while studying philosophy and theology as dogma. In banking education as I had experienced it, the mindset for difficult concepts was "find the truth" in the difficult concept as explained by the textbook. Paulo, on the other hand, was showing me how to think for myself concerning the difficult concepts of "practice" and "contradiction," but what a change in mindset! Thank you, Paulo; you saved my brain. Paulo was a magnificent teacher.

Our "dialogue" was in Spanish, which was a second language for both of us who each had to exert extra effort to communicate and understand. August afternoons were sometimes very warm, and especially on those hot days Paulo's Spanish occasionally became less and less comprehensible. The first time it happened, I asked myself, "what is wrong with my Spanish comprehension that I am grasping less and less?" Eventually I realized that Paulo was unconsciously moving back into Portuguese and occasionally I had to request a return to Spanish. His response was always the same...a smile and "I think I *was* speaking Spanish. Portuguese is almost the same anyway."

At the end of the first week, Paulo handed me a photocopy of the original Portuguese manuscript of *Pedagogy of the Oppressed*. He said, "now it is time to read this and we will discuss it." I said "but it is in Portuguese which I don't know." He said, "I don't have a Spanish version and the translation into English is barely begun. Your Spanish is good so you can learn to read Portuguese in a couple of days with the many Spanish cognates." I thought, "a new language in a couple of days?..Very doubtful." He continued with other encouraging words that showed he had complete confidence that I would be able to do it. Here was a small example of Paulo's gift of having confidence in other people.

Moreover, he was right. With a new Portuguese-English dictionary in hand, and some time spent on the grammar of Portuguese pronouns and several irregular verbs, I was actually reading the first chapter of *Pedagogy of the Oppressed* and was ready to discuss it at our Monday afternoon meeting. I never would have been able to do it without his encouragement, high expectations and my need to have something to start the dialogue on Monday morning. The structure of the tutorial was as promised. He suggested readings, but I was expected to guide the tutorial session with my own questions. Looking back on it, I realized that I as the "educatee" was choosing the themes to be discussed. Willy-nilly I was choosing them because of their meaningfulness to me, and Paulo would wait until he heard what was significant to me before he "problem posed" fulfilling his "educator" role in our tutorial hour. At the time, however, I didn't think of it is educator-educatee dialogue or problem posing. It felt like the most natural of conversations with a very smart and creative man. Paulo was a man whose actions, even in such a thing as my single-person tutorial, were consistent with his theory of education and praxis.

After the first week, Paulo invited me every day to have "onces" with him after the tutorial was over. "Onces" is a Chilean-Spanish word which means something like "snack." At the end of my "hour" we would walk back to the breakfast nook and have fresh coffee with white bread toast, butter and jam. Elza, Paulo's first wife (may she rest in peace), presented the snack, which included what, for me, was an exotic clear glass coffeepot which had a plunger to separate the grounds from the coffee and water. There was a certain ritualistic element in plunging the coffee grounds at the right moment. I assumed it was a Brazilian invention, since I had never seen one before. That conclusion was wrong, but the whole snack culture and conversation seemed transported from Brazil and Chile. This snack time featuring caffeine and toast showed me Paulo's wonderful way of making a guest feel welcome and part of the family. He was a loving man. He had great conversational gifts and was funny, upbeat and optimistic.

In the early 1970s Paulo worked for the World Council of Churches in Geneva. I visited him there and discovered something about his Brazilianness while living in a foreign country as a political exile from Brazil. The dictators considered Freire's literacy work to be too dangerous to allow him to live in his own country.

During my visit with Paulo in Switzerland, he expressed some discontent with the Geneva rules for having friends over for a party. To have a party, one had to inform the other dwellers in one's apartment building, get a permit from the police, and the party itself had to be over by 10:30 p.m. Paulo said, "for us a party doesn't even begin until after 10:30 p.m." During the same visit Paulo asked me to drive his new Peugeot station wagon to a nearby and very beautiful lakeside district. This car was a recent purchase and the older children had not yet learned to drive, and neither Paulo nor Elza had a license, so I was the driver. It was a beautiful day.

We had lunch in a sidewalk café. I remember the warmth and congeniality while spending recreation time with the whole Freire family and enjoying that consistent Paulo Freire lovingness which even included me. One charming and surprising thing about that little trip was being able to observe Paulo at rest. He napped in the back seat during most of the "Sunday drive."

At a conference several years later, I encountered the new and skinny Paulo who, in the meantime, had become interested in healthy eating and regular exercise. No more "onces" with toast and jam! In many writings and in my tutorial he had discussed the possibility of choice between an orientation to life or an orientation to death. Even concerning his own diet and exercise he was committed to life and succeeded in living for many more years.

A professor in my Ph.D. program once warned me against doing a thesis on Freire. He thought the academic world too often produced brilliant stars who were then eclipsed and rapidly forgotten. He worried that this might be the fate of Freire. His advice was, no doubt, true for some academics, but even in 1969 I knew Paulo Freire was a giant who would be considered important for a very long time. I believed this was true partly because of his ability to synthesize elements of pedagogical method, European continental philosophy, a Marxist critique of economic and social inequality, psychology, history and knowledge from other quarters, but mostly because he had put those ideas into practice in Brazil before 1964 and Chile in 1964–68, and the São Paulo school system after 1980. Great theory! Great practice! It was his successful permanent practice which convinced me that his "star" would not set. And it hasn't

In the more than ten years since his death, his work has continued to grow. This growth is a demonstration of his greatness, but I and many others who knew him remember him most as the congruent man who lived every day in such a manner where there was no distance between his everyday life and the ideals he taught.

John McFadden, Retired Professor
Department of Bilingual/Multicultural Education
California State University, Sacramento, California

FROM THE 1970s

Budd L. Hall

Denis E. Collins

BUDD L. HALL

5. SURF ON, PAULIÑO

In the year of Paulo's 70th birthday, the New York City education and social change community hosted a wonderful conference to celebrate his birthday and his contributions to education. The event was so exciting and moving for me that I wrote a poem in his honour and made it available one year after he passed away. I include that poem at the end of these remarks. The title of my remarks, however, comes from the story that Paulo told at the beginning of his talk. He told the assembled throngs in the Art Nouveau Assembly Hall of the New School for Social Research of what he described as the best gift that he had received for his 70th birthday. He said that a young boy in Recife, his home, had given him a picture that he had drawn himself by hand of an old man with a white beard riding on a surf board. At the bottom of the picture, the caption read, "Surf On Pauliño." Paulo laughed as he described the picture and the entire room laughed with him. Paulo said that he intended to keep on going, and he did. It was my pleasure to be able to know and work with Paulo on an off for over 25 years. I met him first in Dar es Salaam and was with him last at the Earth Summit in 1992, where we were both on the plenary panel in the "Educational Tent" in the NGO Forum section of the Earth Summit. In the intervening years I was with him several times in Tanzania, for a summer course in 1975 in Toronto, Ontario at the Ontario Institute for Studies in Education, at several sessions with him in Amherst, Massachusetts organized by my friend Peter Park, in Buenos Aires and elsewhere when he served as Honourary President of the International Council for Adult Education.

I still remember seeing my first copy of the Penguin edition of *Pedagogy of the Oppressed* in the living room of the home of Marjorie Mbilinyi in Dar es Salaam, Tanzania in 1970. Marjorie and I were very excited that a scholar had written such a powerful book about the political and transformative potential of education and using examples from literacy and adult education. He gave voice to the work in which Marjorie, myself and so many others in Tanzania and around the world were engaged, linking learning and political action. He gave us a theoretical platform and a discursive structure with which we could go forth in our meetings and our papers to strengthen the role of education and learning in the transformative movements of our times. No other single book before or since had that kind of electric impact of *Pedagogy of the Oppressed*. I remember him telling me a story later that he had given Penguin permission to reproduce *Pedagogy of the Oppressed* as a paperback without formally clearing the project with the original publishers of the hardcover edition. His only interest was getting the book out cheaply to as many people around the world as possible.

T. Wilson, P. Park and A. Colón-Muñiz (eds.), Memories of Paulo, 21–26.
© 2010 Sense Publishers. All Rights Reserved.

Not long after that, I got word from the Maryknoll Sisters that they were bringing Paulo to Tanzania for three weeks. I was asked by the Director of the Institute of Adult Education to be responsible for his visit while in Tanzania. I was overjoyed. I first met Paulo in the Senate Chambers of the University of Dar es Salaam at a welcoming reception. I walked into the room–there were few of us in the room at the beginning. I saw a quite distinguished-looking gentleman with a brown suit and a tie standing there. It was Paulo! I don't know what I was expecting, perhaps a more radical looking guy with longer hair and wilder eyes? By dressing in this formal way, he was paying respect to the University of Dar es Salaam and the Tanzanian academics that had been waiting to see him. He told the younger people who took over the tasks of taking him around everywhere that it was his birthday…that he was 50 years old. He told us how much Tanzania reminded him of Northeast Brazil and how much he missed the *Fechoada* , the bean dish of his home. At the time he was living in exile in Geneva, Switzerland working as the Education Secretary of the World Council of Churches. He was traveling everywhere sharing his stories about the pedagogies of liberation, hope and transformation.

When it became safe for Paulo and Elza to return to Brazil, Francisco Vio Grossi, who was the Secretary-General of the Latin American Council for Adult Education, and I thought that we should pay a visit to him back in São Paulo where he had settled upon return. He and Elza invited Pancho and me for lunch. He had an apartment with a small balcony and a view over the city and a large dining room with a huge dark table where the family and friends shared stories I imagined on so many occasions. Pancho and I were thrilled to be invited to his home for a meal. Paulo invited us to relax for a moment in the sitting room beneath the window overlooking the city. The sitting room was next to the door of a small patio and near a hanging bird cage just over our heads. Pancho began with some flowery words of welcome from the adult and popular education movement of Latin America. I followed with some elaborate expressions of gratitude on behalf of the global adult education movement. Before I had finished rolling out my discursive flourishes, he held his finger to his lips and said, "Please, not too much noise or you will disturb the canary," as he pointed to the cage above our heads.

His warmth, his kindness in welcoming us into his home, his modesty and nice way of bringing us back down to a level of friendship from one of adulation was typical. Paulo had a magical quality of connecting to people, of extending his friendship to others. I saw him do it with groups of Zanzibar women, with popular educators in Europe and Asia, and with academic groups in the United States in many places. He loved us, all of us. And we loved him in return.

I had the privilege of introducing Paulo Freire to Julius K Nyerere, then President of the Republic of Tanzania. President Nyerere (Mwalimu or Teacher as he was called) had read *Pedagogy of the Oppressed*. Freire knew the writings of Nyerere well and had tremendous respect for his leadership. Mwalimu Nyerere wanted to know why, if the purpose of *Pedagogy of the Oppressed* was education for liberation, he had written it in such a dense academic style? I heard that question many times over the years in Paulo's company and he answered it differently later in life, but on that day he replied to President Nyerere that at the time of writing *Pedagogy of the Oppressed*, he was still too caught up in the identity of the academic and scholar. He suggested that had he known the popularity and purposes that the book was to be used for in so many countries, he might have written it differently. He asked Mwalimu Nyerere whether Tanzania would welcome some kind of international centre based on his ideas. Paulo said that there were many people around the world that were interested in his ideas, but that there wasn't a centre where more sustained research and study could be done. Nyerere replied that Tanzania would welcome such a centre. In the end, this never came to be, but not because of any lack of interest on either Freire or Nyerere's sides.

One of the stories that I love was one from 1985 in Argentina. Raul Alfonsin had just been elected President of Argentina, bringing to an end one of the most brutal military dictatorships of the 20th century. Intellectuals and political activists had been killed in the thousands, "disappeared" in the parlance of the day. The International Council for Adult Education (ICAE) wished to hold its next world assembly in Buenos Aires in November of 1985. So we organized a meeting of the Executive Committee of the Latin American Council for Adult Education to meet in June of 1985. Paulo, as Honourary President of ICAE, was invited to help with the planning for the forthcoming World Assembly of Adult Education. *Pedagogy of the Oppressed* had been a book that was banned during the military dictatorship. To be found with a copy was a crime. Isabel Hernandez, the great Argentine popular educator, was the conference organizer for the World Assembly and was having trouble getting support from the Argentinean government. The political party which controlled the Ministry of Education did not share an interest in popular education and was an obstacle to getting the word out that a major gathering of world adult educators was coming to Buenos Aires.

Isabel had the idea that we could hold a public forum on popular education making use of Paulo's popularity and then provide information on the forthcoming World Assembly, thereby getting directly to the people of Buenos Aires and bypassing the Ministry reluctance. Isabel proposed the idea. We thought it brilliant. All except for Paulo. He said that he did not like to speak in such large settings. We begged him to please consider it because we needed the visibility that only he could bring. He finally agreed but only on the condition that Isabel, Francisco Vio Grossi and myself speak first on the panel. And then he said that he would only speak for ten minutes. We were thrilled and as we worked during the afternoon in one of the meeting rooms of the Centre San Martin, we noticed that by 3 and 4 in the afternoon people were already streaming into the main assembly hall. Such was the hunger for democratic discussions in a country recovering from years of brutality and hopelessness. By 8 pm, the time of the talk, the entire 1200-seat Assembly of the Centro San Martin was filled and the windows alongside the one wall of the Assembly Hall were packed with people who could not get in. Paulo was a rock star!

We worked our way around to the back stage of the Assembly Hall though a series of secretive corridors. When we entered the stage there was an explosion of applause as some 1500 people leapt to their feet. Isabel opened the panel with information about the forthcoming World Assembly. I said a few things about adult education and democracy to a muted reception. Francisco Vio Grossi managed a somewhat better appetizer performance and then it was time for Paulo. Paulo stood shyly in the bright lights as if wondering what he was to say. He then caught the eye of an old friend from Buenos Aires, a friend of many years before, sitting in the front row. They smiled to each other and Paulo began talking about how precious was this moment of return to Buenos Aires now that democracy had come back. He spoke of the meaning of the words "Buenos" and "Aires" and moved into a conversation with the room on the meaning of love. It was the most beautiful and moving talk that I ever heard him give. He drew inspiration from the energies of the crowd, from the energies of the moment, from the democratic aspirations of so many and played these energies back through his words to our open hearts and minds. He spoke for nearly an hour and seemed to be gaining strength as he went along.

It is hard to believe that he has been gone from us physically for over ten years. In a way, however, Paulo is someone who will never leave us. His ideas, his love for all of us, his passion for ordinary people and his ability to link educational practice to transformative change, is brought to life each time we read one of his books, listen to one of his talks and talk with others about his ideas.

For me personally, it was one of the great honours in my life to have been able to have some time with him, to be able to support his vision and to know his influence in so many parts of the world.

SURF ON PAULIÑO[1]

Lire les mots
Lire les textes
Lire les vies
Lire le monde
Lire nos coeurs

I mean picture this:
600 street-wise American and Canadian activists
Assembled in the conference hall of the
New School of Social Research in New York City
Where in 1932 the first North American meeting of the
Workers Education Association was held

A birthday conference for Paulo Freire, the most influential
Educational thinker of the 20th century
Academics jammed in next to homeless organizers who are
Jammed in next to Lady Garment Workers who are
Jammed in next to the Puerto Rican Independence underground who are
Jammed in next to kindergarten teachers who are
Jammed in next to high school students who are
Waiting to hear from Paulo Freire

And Paulo, 70 years old, who has come to town to help us all
Celebrate ourselves through him, stands up behind a table on the
Stage

"I'd like to tell you,"
 Paulo says in his quiet gentle voice,
"About the best gift that I have had for my birthday.
I received it from a young boy in Recife, in Northeast Brazil where
I was born.
He gave me the gift of a picture which he had drawn himself
A picture of the crashing Atlantic coastal waves
And in the picture was a man riding on what I think is called a
Surf board.
And on top of the board, riding the waves, was an old man with a
White beard and glasses.
That old man was me. It was a picture of me.
And my young friend had written words beneath this picture in his
Own handwriting.
He told me 'Surf On Pauliño'
Surf on little Paulo
"And," Paulo said with a smile that reached out to the entire hall,
"I intend to do just that."

For Paulo was a transcendent rider of the waves
Waves of respect for the oppressed people of this planet
Waves of intellectual curiosity; lover of words
Waves of exile and loneliness in Chile, Geneva and Africa
Waves of love for his children, his dear Elza who died before him
Waves of love for the final love of his life, his widow Nita.
And waves of love for his friends in such places as Guinea-Bissau,
Cuba, India, Fiji, France and, yes, for us in Canada.

For if he was a teacher
For if he was an activist
For if he was a writer
For if he was a teller of stories
He was above all a person in the great and ancient tradition of
Brazilian mystics
More than a teacher
More than an activist
More than a writer
More than the teller of stories

He carried with him a warm breeze of historic possibility
He carried with him the memories of many struggles
He carried with him vulnerability and need
He carried with him opportunities for friendship
He carried with him the new eyes of the young
He carried with him revolutionary agency
He carried with him his hand for ours

He carried with him the electric atmosphere of a Northeastern
Brazilian Storm

Paulo often apologized for his ways of speaking languages other
Than his beloved Portuguese
And yet he held audiences at hushed attention when he spoke in
English, French or Spanish in every corner of the world
He found ways through his distinct ways of speaking English and
French and other languages to draw us in to his speech
To draw us into himself
So much did he seem to need us, his audience, that we hung onto his
Every word and we helped him to reach out to ourselves

So that in the end
We were his text
We were his words
He was our text
He was our words

Nous étions ses mots
Nous étions son texte
Il était notre texte
Il était nos mots

Lire les mots
Lire les textes
Lire les vies
Lire le monde
Lire nos coeurs

Pauliño
Surf on

NOTES

[1]   Written by Budd L Hall for Paulo's birthday, one year after he passed away.

REFERENCE

Freire, P. (2000). *Pedagogy of the oppressed.* London: Continuum International Press.

Budd L Hall
Office of Community-Based Research
University of Victoria, Canada

DENIS E. COLLINS

6. SEATTLE, JANUARY 1973

I was privileged to meet Paulo Freire in January 1973. During the previous summer, in order to lower travel costs, I had taken a job driving an émigré's car from Southern California to Toronto where I then traveled by train and auto to Washington, D.C. The occasion was a chance to see and hear Freire in person at an advertised panel presentation at American University. When I arrived in Washington, I learned to my chagrin that his appearance had been cancelled. Because the trip had been interesting and included a chance to tour some colonial sites in the Chesapeake area, my disappointment was checked, but frustrating nevertheless.

At that time I had completed several months working in Mexico where I had collected many documents containing a great deal of Freire's work not yet translated into English. The previous May I had also visited Ohio State University where Anne Hartung and John Ohliger had invited me to share my Mexican findings and peruse their resources collected for E.R.I.C. over a period of some eighteen months. Those documents included many of the first North American reactions to Freire based largely on two articles in the *Harvard Educational Review* and his first English edition of *Pedagogy of the Oppressed*. With these materials in hand I was about to start writing my dissertation, *Two Utopians: A Comparison and Contrast of the Educational Philosophies of Paulo Freire and Theodore Brameld*. (University of Southern California, 1973)

On a late summer hike I told a companion, Father Ed Murphy of our China Province, about my disappointment in missing Freire at Washington. How great was my delight when after two months of writing I received a letter from Ed inviting me to a meeting with Paulo at Seattle University! At the January meeting Freire would address representatives from the ten U.S. Jesuit Provinces who were involved with funding and supervision of American Jesuits sent to work outside the U.S. The purpose of the meeting was to continue updating contemporary thinking about "missionary" activity and whatever that might mean in the wake of the Second Vatican Council. By that time Freire was already hard at work in Geneva where he served the World Council of Churches as head of their Education Secretariat.

I kept hard at my writing throughout the autumn, jotting down a number of questions I wanted to pose to Freire and the great day came when I flew to Seattle to hear him in person. I was able to attend an open meeting with him that first night on the University of Washington campus and joined graduate students and

T. Wilson, P. Park and A. Colón-Muñiz (eds.), Memories of Paulo, 27–29.

professors from all over the Northwest who packed a lecture hall for the evening. My initial impression was pleasure and admiration for his affable manner and dedication to all the issues he addressed. We were made painfully aware that Richard Nixon was still in office, the Vietnam War was raging years after the Tet Offensive, and Freire still felt obligated to ask us not to tape record his remarks. Watergate and the overthrow of Allende were still months away, but the intimidation of Kissinger, the CIA, and others reached across the UW campus that evening.

The next morning I was invited to ride with an Oregon Jesuit to collect Freire and his wife Elza at a dorm on the UW campus. The venue of the back seat of a Volkswagen gave me opportunity for a private interview where Freire graciously and patiently answered my questions as we rode up and down the Seattle hills. He was extremely interested and helpful. When I told him I was probably going to work with Jesuit educators in the U.S. and I asked him (not so naively as the reader might suspect) whether he thought we could ever implement his educational philosophy in Jesuit schools in this country, he reached over, put a hand on my knee, and smilingly replied, "Not until you succeed in overthrowing your government." Either prudence or cowardice kept me from including that response in my dissertation, but I have never been unmindful of his reply!

Throughout that morning, Freire listened to about thirty Jesuits and, with great kindness and honesty, answered their questions and gave his advice. His audience was more than empathetic with his exhortations to avoid the mistakes of centuries past regarding the oppressors' tactic of cultural invasion he had criticized so well in the fourth chapter of *Pedagogy of the Oppressed.* We finished at noon and you can imagine my delight when the VW driver tossed me the keys and said, "You can take Paulo back to the dorm." I immediately invited him and Elza to lunch. I made that invitation in the presence of several Jesuit seminarians who had come over from Spokane to hear Freire, and they quickly pressured me to invite them along too. Thank God for plastic, so that we had a delightful, convenient meal with the Freires where Paulo regaled us with obvious amusement along the lines of his now famous *Carta a un Joven Teologo* (1972) that set forth his ideal description of priests who could serve people best by going through the "Easter experience" as he suggested for anyone daring to embark on implementation of dialogical problem posing pedagogy.

When I returned these two gentle Brazilians to their dorm quarters, Paulo invited me up to their room where he put into my hands a copy of the pamphlet most recently published by his adult children with him in exile at I.D.A.C., "The Oppression of Pedagogy and the Pedagogy of the Oppressed." Graciously, he autographed the copy for me and sent me back to California with a head full of ideas and a heart full of gratitude for his generosity during that visit.

It was nearly thirty years later upon the publication of *Pedagogy of Hope* (1992) where I learned for the first time how rudely he and Elza had been treated earlier on their 1973 visit to their hotel restaurant in Chicago. In the mid-1990s I was horrified and embarrassed for my countrymen at Chicago, grateful that maybe in just some small way over soup and sandwiches and a ride back to their dorm at Seattle I had been able to offer a moment of hospitality to these two wonderful people and appreciate their kindness.

REFERENCES

Freire, P. (1998). *Pedagogy of hope: Reliving pedagogy of the oppressed.* London: Continuum International Publishing Group, Ltd.
Freire, P. (1972). *Letter to a theology student.* Contacto, IX. No.1.

Denis E. Collins, S.J.: Santa Barbara, California

FROM THE 1980s

Sonia Nieto
Peter Park
Mary Brydon-Miller
Henry A. Giroux
Peggy Rivage-Seul
Manuel N. Gómez
Ronald David Glass
Patricia Gómez
Michael W. Apple
Tom Wilson
Anaida Colon-Muñiz
Ira Shor
Terri Egan
Brook Larios
Cesar Rossatto
Herbert Bernstein
Rudolfo Chávez-Chávez
Mark Lynd
John Rivera
Robert W. Howard
Tom Sticht
Helen M. Lewis
Esther Pérez
Luis Fuentes

SONIA NIETO

7. EATING *TOSTONES* AND CHANGING LIVES

My fondest memory of Paulo Freire is this: it is 1981 and he is sitting at my dining room table and my daughter Marisa, then six years old, is on his lap as he enjoys a Puerto Rican dinner that I cooked in his honor. He tells me how much he enjoys the dinner–chicken with rice, red beans, *tostones* (fried plantains), salad, *flan*– and that it reminds him of home, his beloved Brazil, from which he was still exiled. I remember this image fondly because it epitomizes Paulo Freire, the human being, who, in the midst of his musings on the political nature of education, also wrote, "I love children. I may be wrong, but I think children also love me a lot."[1] And he was right: children loved him a lot, as did adults of all ages and backgrounds.

I think it's important to cherish these images of humanity and personal connection because without them, we are apt to focus on the myth or the legend rather than on the man. With Paulo, it was normal to feel that one was in the presence of great-ness when he was around. It was easy to make a legend of Paulo; he was colossal in his ideas and his impact. Yet, besides his monumental intellectual stature, he was above all else a very human being. He was funny and he loved a good meal; he got angry and he laughed; he treasured his family and he missed his homeland.

Although he died more than ten years ago, Paulo Freire continues to change the world with his ideas. He certainly changed the world for me. The first time I read *Pedagogy of the Oppressed* was in 1975, the year I became a doctoral student. The book spoke to me in a way that no other book ever had. When I read it, I had already taught in various contexts–elementary and middle school classrooms in New York City, a community-based ESL program, the Puerto Rican Studies Department at Brooklyn College–and it seemed to me that Freire's text was just as relevant in those contexts, although perhaps in different ways, as it was in Brazil or in the developing countries in Latin America and Africa where his work had been, and continues to be, most influential. I have returned to *Pedagogy of the Oppressed* many times since my first reading in 1975, and it is always enlightening and challenging, but it was during that first reading that I was awakened to ideas that until then had been dormant in me. This text became a transformative one in my development as a scholar, teacher educator, and researcher.

Imagine, then, how thrilled I was, as a newly minted professor at the University of Massachusetts in 1980, to find out that Paulo Freire was to be a Visiting Scholar on our campus. I immediately volunteered to be a member of the planning committee for his month-long visit, the first of four or five he would make in the coming years. The faculty, students, and staff on the committee organized seminars, talks in classes, receptions, public appearances, and visits to the various communities

T. Wilson, P. Park and A. Colón-Muñiz (eds.), Memories of Paulo, 33–34.

surrounding Amherst. We also arranged for breakfasts, lunches, and dinners for Paulo and Elza, his first wife, and it was especially during these occasions that we got to know not only the ideas, but also the person. It was at one of these dinners that Marisa ended up sitting on Paulo's lap.

Paulo was in his late 50s at the time, but he was timeless. No matter his age, Paulo was always young–in ideas, in temperament, in how he faced life. His appearance did not change very much from the time I met him until his death nearly two decades later: a white beard, kind and wise eyes, tweed jackets and homemade sweaters. What I remember most is his voice: melodic, thoughtful, choosing his words carefully, and asking whoever spoke Portuguese or Spanish around him to help translate. This is how I ended up on stage with him one night in an auditorium at the U Mass in the early 1980s. He really did not need me there to help him with English–he spoke it eloquently–but rather to have a face with which to engage because, for him, to dialogue meant having a personal conversation even if it were among hundreds of participants.

Paulo always seemed to have his hand on someone's shoulder; he needed to connect with whomever he was speaking, be it the president of a university or a community worker, with a man or a woman, a young student or a senior scholar. Perhaps this is why his ideas always resonated with me: when I read his words, I imagine him sitting there, speaking with me, his hand on my shoulder, helping me make sense of the world, pushing me to be courageous in my thinking, in my teaching, in my writing, and in my life.

NOTES

[1] Freire, P. (1985). *The politics of education: Culture, Power, and Liberation.* South Hadley, MA: Bergin & Garvey, p. 197

Sonia Nieto, Professor Emerita
School of Education
University of Massachusetts, Amherst

PETER PARK

8. FRAGMENTS OF MEMORY

Paulo Freire

With all the fame that accrued to him throughout the world, Paulo was still a down-to-earth person and never let the fame and the celebrity he enjoyed swell his head. He was very much a man of the mundane world, enjoying ordinary things and not allowing his status to put himself above ordinary folks. Above all he was never afraid of making fun of himself.

Paulo came to the University of Massachusetts, where I was teaching, as a visiting professor for a month for three years in a row soon after returning to Brazil from his exile in Switzerland. The first year he was there, he received quite unex-pectedly an invitation from the governor of the state of São Paulo to attend a ceremony in São Paulo at which he would be honored for his achievement in education. The invitation came after he had just arrived in the States and by this time he was joined by some of his family members–his two sons and a daughter as well as his first wife, Elza. And he had just started getting engaged with the academic activities on campus which had been worked out for him, giving lectures and seminars and attending meetings, and so forth. He explained the situation to the governor saying that it is difficult for him to get away because of his schedule at the university. The governor asked him to change the schedule in view of the importance of the occasion. Paulo replied that it would be difficult since he was dealing with the people, meaning Americans, who "invented schedule." But in the end the governor prevailed and he was able to rearrange the schedule so he could attend the ceremony in São Paulo. On this occasion, the governor recognized achievements in various fields, including the sciences, the humanities, and the arts and there were other notables receiving the awards at the same time. Upon returning to the states from the ceremony, he tells this story of meeting a well-known Brazilian popular singer, Gal Costa, backstage. Paulo was a big fan of Gal Costa and he was excited to meet her for the first time in person. So, upon seeing her he stuck out his hand to her and introduced himself, saying, "I am Paulo Freire." To which, she replied, "Who?" He would tell this story with a twinkle in his eyes and much humility.

Paulo loved to eat good food, not necessarily fancy food, but well prepared and tasty food. One time, he came to visit me in Berkeley, where I was spending a year on a research project. He was lecturing at Stanford. Since his visit was at lunch time, I asked him what he would like to eat. He said he had a hankering for a turkey sandwich on white bread. I had some difficulty finding a restaurant that

T. Wilson, P. Park and A. Colón-Muñiz (eds.), Memories of Paulo, 35–37.

served white bread in the environs of the university at the time and we ended up settling for French bread. I didn't think this was quite what he had in mind, but he ate it seemingly with pleasure. I was worried because I remembered the time when he attended a dinner meeting at Smith College. I noticed that he didn't touch the roasted chicken that was on his plate. He later explained to me that the chicken in the States is not "real" chicken. I appreciated this sentiment later when I visited Brazil and tasted the free-ranging chicken served there, which was very tasty and quite different from the industrial variety found in the States. In many ways, he was accommodating and easy going about things, but he was discriminating in his taste, as was firm about what he would accept or not accept without being offensive about it. In this respect, his philosophy, which is well grounded and embracive but not compromising on key issues, mirrors his daily life.

While he was in Massachusetts we would often go out to eat in restaurants. But once in a while Elza, Paulo's first wife, would cook. One time, Elza taught me how to cook red snapper Brazilian style, which resembles a Mexican dish which we sometimes call Veracruzana in this country. It is cooked slowly with tomatoes, green peppers, onions, and olives in olive oil and topped off with cilantro. But once in a while I would invite them to dinner and cook for them. On these occasions we would talk about how we appreciated good food and say that we should start a restaurant. But invariably, Paulo would finish the conversation by saying that we would never make any money since we would end up giving away food to friends. This is as far as our scheme to open up a restaurant would go. Once, I decided to make spaghetti amatriciana. Paulo was in the kitchen when I was preparing the food. He asked me what was in the sauce. When I explained, he asked me if I could modify the recipe by adding chopped raw onions at the last minute. I resisted this request saying I had never seen amatriciana served this way. But he gently insisted and I gave in. So I sprinkled chopped raw onions on the pasta which was mixed with the amatriciana sauce. The result was a surprisingly delicious dish, which in some ways was an improvement on the original amatriciana recipe. I ended up calling this spaghetti amatriciana a la Paulo Freire. I sometimes make this dish now and serve it to friends, who are often skeptical at first but then seem to enjoy it. I remember telling this story to some friends in Cuba, all admirers of Paulo, who got curious about the dish and asked me to cook it for them. I foolishly accepted the invitation and proceeded to prepare the meal without quite realizing the challenges it would pose in obtaining the necessary ingredients and working with limited kitchen facilities. But that is another story.

In 1986, I was in Brazil for a series of talks with universities and institutes to arrange an exchange program involving the University of Massachusetts and these institutions. On this occasion I spent a few days visiting with Paulo in São Paulo. It was a year of the World Cup and there was a great deal of excitement in Brazil. I arrived in São Paulo on the day Brazil was playing France in the final game. On the way to the city from the airport, I noticed that the streets were eerily quiet and once in awhile I would see flickering of television lights through the windows lining the streets. And once I settled into the lodging where I was staying and trying to take a little nap, I would hear shouts of "Goal!" coming from neighboring rooms.

Unfortunately for Brazil, however, it lost the game and the Cup with it. The next day I went to visit Paulo in his house and found him in a deep depression. He was feeling so dejected about the loss that he was barely in the mood to talk. Apparently he was unable to eat as well. This state was to last a couple of days.

One summer when Paulo and I were both in southern California, I arranged to go to a baseball game with Paulo, Nita, Paulo's second wife whom he married after being widowed by Elza, and my wife Kathleen. The Dodgers were playing in LA. I picked up the Freires and drove to the Dodgers stadium. Having arrived there a little late, I parked the car in a hurry without noticing the location where I was parking and we proceeded to our seats. Baseball was a new experience for Paulo and Nita. I sat next to Paulo and tried to explain the rules of the game to Paulo and Nita as best as I could. But once in awhile, I would hear Paulo whispering to Nita that he couldn't understand what was going on. But he sat through the whole thing patiently, including the seventh inning stretch which was a complete mystery to him. We decided to leave before the end of the ninth inning in order to beat the traffic. Upon arriving at the parking lot, I realized I had no idea where I had left the car. We all four walked around the parking lot looking for the car for a long time in a futile search. By this time the game let out and swarms of cars were moving, which made the task very difficult. We then decided to wait until all the cars had left. By this time it was getting late and we were all very hungry. Throughout this ordeal, Paulo did not murmur a word of complaint, waiting very patiently with calmness which astounded me and at the same time reassured me. He didn't show any signs of being bothered by the experience. I then realized how he practiced his own pedagogical advice in daily life. He used to say that we have to be "patiently impatient" to see our dreams of a more just world become reality.

Peter Park, Professor Emeritus
University of Massachusetts, Amherst

MARY BRYDON-MILLER

9. THE GIFTS OF THE MAGUS

In Remembrance of Paulo Freire

I have three gifts given to me by Paulo Freire. The first is, of all things, a purse. It's a summery sort of purse, light gray and beige stripes with wooden beads hanging from the ends of the strap. I had served as a kind of informal assistant to Paulo during his time to the University of Massachusetts, and Elza told him that this would be an appropriate thank-you gift for a young woman, so the two of us went dutifully down to the local shopping mall to pick one out together. Those who know me probably don't think of me as much of a purse person, but I take an almost absurd delight in owning it because I believe it was given with genuine affection.

The other two gifts are short volumes of poetry by Ernesto Cardenal. In signing them, Paulo tells me to "be in peace with his poems." I reread Cardenal's words as I began writing this remembrance, and found it impossible to "be in peace" with these poems of passion and apocalypse, work intended to provoke and stir one to action. Instead, I find that I am thankful to Paulo for giving me these books because, years later, they continue to evoke a sense of restlessness and demand my engagement in the world.

But the most deeply cherished gifts I received from Paulo, the ones I am sure many of us share, are gifts of the heart. A few of them are gratefully recognized here.

A DEEP, ABIDING, AND SUSTAINING REVERENCE FOR THE HUMAN SPIRIT

Paulo brought to every interaction an absolute authenticity and openness, a conviction that he would learn something new and important from every person he encountered. You could see it in the way he leaned forward eagerly when listening to someone speak, in the intensity with which he attended to what was being said, and in his respect for the intellect and experience of the speaker. Knowing you were truly being heard, gave you the courage to speak.

A FEROCIOUS, DEMANDING LOVE: LOVE AS "AN ACT OF COURAGE"

Antonia Darder talks about experiencing this same quality in her book *Reinventing Freire: A Pedagogy of Love,* noting "his enormous capacity to love and to extend himself as a full human being." I think of this as the love Christ really had in mind for us all to show one another, a love that requires us to challenge oppression and injustice.

T. Wilson, P. Park and A. Colón-Muñiz (eds.), Memories of Paulo, 39–41.

WISDOM, INTELLIGENCE, AND AN INSATIABLE CURIOSITY

When I first read Freire as a graduate student, I was particularly struck by the breadth of his knowledge of diverse disciplines. Coming from the field of psychology where the majority of scholarship seemed to narrow rather than to expand our thinking, encountering this expansiveness gave me permission to explore. But at the same time, he always made it clear that intellect must be accompanied by the humility and patience required to nurture it. Learning begins with the admission of ignorance and many of us are so guarded against this that it makes it impossible to be open to new ideas and new ways of understanding the world. There is a sense of vulnerability, of nakedness, in admitting that we do not know. This never seemed to worry Paulo, allowing him to be always an eager student.

ANIMATION, AFFECTION, AND A VIBRANT ENTHUSIASM FOR LIFE

Even sitting at a conference table he seemed barely contained, his hands always moving, his eyes taking in everything and everyone in the room. Paulo had a wry and sometimes mischievous sense of humor. Like his friend, Myles Horton, he was a marvelous storyteller, and often the stories provoked both laughter and learning. And his warmth–unselfconsciously expressed in a touch, a hand on a shoulder or an embrace–established a kind of covenant of respect and caring among those with whom he worked.

ANGER AND A SENSE OF OUTRAGE

In *Pedagogy of the City*, Paulo referred to this as "the necessary anger and the indispensable indignation" that gave him the courage to battle oppression. But his was an anger always tempered by hopefulness. He had the absolute conviction that change is possible, without the naiveté to think it would be easy nor the arrogance to think that it could be done alone.

AN UNSTINTING WILLINGNESS TO SHARE THESE GIFTS WITH OTHERS

Those of us who knew Paulo know that we were indeed blessed to be granted this enduring legacy. But his generosity of spirit was accompanied by the clear expectation that we would in turn strive to pass these same gifts along to our own students, colleagues, and community partners.

I am fortunate now, and profoundly grateful, to see these same gifts embodied in the work of my own students. Teachers, school and community leaders, physical and mental health care professionals–they daily demonstrate the same sense of commitment to bringing about positive change in the lives of those with whom they work. They reflect the same respect for others, the same curiosity and eagerness for learning, and the same sense of outrage mingled with hopefulness that lives in Paulo's words. Witnessing their dedication I know that his legacy is in good hands.

You came to visit me in dreams
but the emptiness you left behind when you went away
was real.

Epigrams, Ernesto Cardenal

REFERENCES

Cardenal, E. (1975). *Apocalypse and other poems*. New York: New Directions Books.
Darder, A. (2002). *Reinventing Paulo Freire: A pedagogy of love*. Boulder, CO: Westview Press.
Freire, P. (2000). Pedagogy of the city: The challenges of Urban education. In Ana Maria Araújo Freire & Donaldo Macedo (Eds.), *The Paulo Freire Reader* (pp. 231–236). New York: Continuum.

Mary Brydon-Miller, Associate Professor
Educational Studies and Urban Educational Leadership
University of Cincinnati, Cincinnati, Ohio

HENRY A. GIROUX

10. PAULO FREIRE

Reconnecting the Personal and the Political

I first met Paulo in the early 1980s, just after I had been denied tenure by John Silber, the President of Boston University. Paulo was giving a talk at the University of Massachusetts and he came to my house in Boston for dinner. His humility was completely at odds with his reputation and I remember being greeted with such warmth and sincerity that I felt completely at ease with him. We talked for a long time that night about his exile, my firing, what it meant to be a working class intellectual, the risk one had to take to make a difference, and when the night was over a friendship was forged that lasted until his death fifteen years later. I was in a very bad place after being denied tenure, and had no idea what my future would hold for me. I am convinced that if it had not been for Paulo and Donaldo Macedo, also a friend of Paulo's, I am not sure I would have stayed in the field of education. Unlike so many intellectuals I have met in academia, Paulo was always so generous, eager to publish the work of younger intellectuals, write letters of support, and give as much of himself as possible in the service of others. The early eighties were exciting years in education in the U.S. and Paulo was at the center of it. Together we started a series at Bergin and Garvey Publishers and published over a hundred young authors, many of whom went on to have a significant influence in the university. Jim Bergin had become Paulo's patron as his American publisher; Donaldo became his translator and a co-author, and we all took our best shots in translating, publishing, and distributing Paulo's work, always with the hope of inviting him back to the U.S. so we could meet, talk, drink good wine, and recharge the struggles that all marked us in different ways. Of course, it is difficult to write simply about Paulo as a person, because who he was, and how he entered one's space and the world, could never be separated from his politics. Hence, I want to try to provide a broader context for my own understanding of him as well as those ideas that consistently shaped our relationship and his relationship with others.

Occupying the in-between space of the political and the possible, Paulo Freire spent most of his life working in the belief that the radical elements of democracy are worth struggling for, that critical education is a basic element of social change, and that how we think about politics is inseparable from how we come to understand the world, power, and the moral life we aspire to lead. In many ways, Paulo embodied the delicate and often problematic relationship between the personal and the political. His own life was a testimonial to not only his belief in democracy, but also to the notion that one's life had to come as close as possible to modeling the

T. Wilson, P. Park and A. Colón-Muñiz (eds.), Memories of Paulo, 43–46.
© *2010 Sense Publishers. All Rights Reserved.*

social relations and experiences that spoke to a more humane and democratic future. At the same time, Paulo never moralized about politics, never employed the discourse of shame, or collapsed the political into the personal when talking about social issues. For him, private problems had to be understood in relation to larger public issues. Everything about him suggested that the first order of politics was humility, compassion, and a willingness to fight against human injustices.

Freire's belief in democracy as well as his deep and abiding faith in the ability of people to resist the weight of oppressive institutions and ideologies was forged in a spirit of struggle tempered by both the grim realities of his own imprisonment and exile, mediated by both a fierce sense of outrage and the belief that education and hope are the conditions of both agency and politics. Acutely aware that many contemporary versions of hope occupied their own corner in a Disneyland culture, Freire fought against such appropriations and was passionate about recovering and rearticulating hope through, in his words, an "understanding of history as opportunity and not determinism."[1] Hope for Freire was a practice of witnessing, an act of moral imagination that enabled progressive educators and others to think otherwise in order to act otherwise, Hope demanded an anchoring in transformative practices, and one of the tasks of the progressive education was to "unveil opportunities for hope, no matter what the obstacles may be."[2] Underlying Freire's politics of hope was a view of radical pedagogy that located itself on the dividing lines where the relations between domination and oppression, power and powerlessness, continued to be produced and reproduced. For Freire, hope as a defining element of politics and pedagogy always meant listening to and working with the poor and other subordinate groups so that they might speak and act in order to alter dominant relations of power. Whenever we talked he never allowed himself to become cynical. He was always full of life, took delight in what it meant to eat a good meal, listen to music, open himself up to new experiences, and engage in dialogue with a passion that both embodied his own politics and confirmed the lived presence of others.

Committed to the specific, the play of context, and the possibility inherent in what he called the unfinished nature of human beings, Freire offered no recipes for those in need of instant theoretical and political fixes. For him, pedagogy was strategic and performative; considered as part of a broader political practice for democratic change, critical pedagogy was never viewed as an a priori discourse to be reasserted or a methodology to be implemented. On the contrary, for Freire pedagogy was a political and performative act organized around the "instructive ambivalence of disrupted borders,"[3] a practice of bafflement, interruption, understanding, and intervention that is the result of ongoing historical, social, and economic struggles. I was often amazed at how patient he always was in dealing with people who wanted him to provide menu-like answers to the problems they raised about education, not realizing that they were undermining his own insistence that pedagogy could never be reduced to a method. His patience was always instructive for me and I am convinced that it was only later in my life that I was able to begin to emulate it in my own interactions with audiences.

Paulo was a cosmopolitan intellectual who never overlooked either the details in everyday life nor the connections the latter had to a much broader, global world. He consistently reminded us that political struggles are won and lost in those specific yet hybridized spaces that linked narratives of everyday experience with the social gravity and material force of institutional power. Any radical pedagogy that called itself Freirean had to acknowledge the centrality of the particular and the contingent in shaping historical contexts and political projects. Although Freire was a theoretician of radical contextualism, he also acknowledged the importance of understanding the particular and the local in relation to larger, global and cross-national forces. For Freire, literacy as a way of reading and changing the world had to be reconceived within a broader understanding of citizenship, democracy, and justice that was global and transnational. Making the pedagogical more political in this case meant moving beyond the celebration of tribal mentalities and developing a praxis that foregrounded "power, history, memory, relational analysis, justice (not just representation), and ethics as the issues central to transnational democratic struggles."[4]

But Freire's insistence that radical education was about the making and changing of contexts did more than seize upon the political and pedagogic potentialities to be found across a spectrum of social sites and practices in society, which of course, included but were not limited to the school. He also challenged the separation of culture from politics by calling attention to how diverse technologies of power work pedagogically within institutions to produce, regulate, and legitimize particular forms of knowing, belonging, feeling, and desiring. But Freire did not make the mistake of many of his contemporaries by conflating culture with the politics of recognition. Politics was more than a gesture of translation, representation and dialogue; it was also about mobilizing social movements against the oppressive economic, racial, and sexist practices put into place by colonization, global capitalism, and other oppressive structures of power.

Paulo Freire left behind a corpus of work that emerged out of a lifetime of struggle and commitment. Refusing the comfort of master narratives, Freire's work was always unsettled and unsettling, restless yet engaging. Unlike so much of the politically arid and morally vacuous academic and public prose that characterizes contemporary intellectual discourse, Freire's work was consistently fueled by a healthy rage over the needless oppression and suffering he witnessed throughout his life as he traveled all over the globe. Similarly, his work exhibited a vibrant and dynamic quality that allowed it to grow, refuse easy formulas, and open itself to new political realities and projects. Freire's genius was to elaborate a theory of social change and engagement that was neither vanguardist nor populist. While he had a profound faith in the ability of ordinary people to shape history and to become critical agents in shaping their own destinies, he refused to romanticize the culture and experiences that produced oppressive social conditions. Combining theoretical rigor, social relevance, and moral compassion, Freire gave new meaning to the politics of daily life while affirming the importance of theory in opening up the space of critique, possibility, politics, and practice. Theory and language were a site of struggle and possibility that gave experience meaning, and action a political direction, and any attempt to reproduce the binarism of theory vs. politics was repeatedly condemned by Freire.[5] Freire loved theory, but he never reified it. When he talked about Freud, Marx, or Erich Fromm, one could feel his intense passion for ideas. And yet he never treated theory as an end to itself; it was always a resource to be used to understand, critically engage, and transform the world. To say that his joy around such matters was infectious is to understand his presence and impact on so many people that he met in his life.

I had a close personal relationship with Paulo for over seventeen years, and I was always moved by the way in which his political courage and intellectual reach were matched by a love of life and generosity of spirit. He once told me that he could not imagine a revolutionary who did not like good food and music. I am not sure if it was the love of food, or music, or maybe both, that allowed his poetry to slip into politics. And as I have mentioned earlier, the political and the personal mutually informed Freire's life and work. He was always the curious student even as he assumed the role of a critical teacher. As he moved between the private and the public, he revealed an astonishing gift for making everyone he met feel valued. His very presence embodied what it meant to combine political struggle and moral courage, to make hope meaningful and despair unpersuasive. Paulo was fond of quoting Che Guevara's adage: "Let me tell you, at the risk of appearing ridiculous, the genuine revolutionary is animated by feelings of love. It is impossible to imagine an authentic revolutionary without this quality."[6] Though it has been more than ten years since his death, I have not met anyone who has embodied this sentiment more than Paulo Freire.

NOTES

[1]   Freire, *Pedagogy of Hope*, p. 91.
[2]   Ibid, *p. 9.*
[3]   Cited in Becker, *The Enchantment of Art*, p. 28.
[4]   Alexander, *Introduction: Genealogies, Legacies, Movements*, p. Xix.
[5]   Surely, Freire would have agreed wholeheartedly with Stuart Hall's insight that: "It is only through the way in which we represent and imagine ourselves that we come to know how we are constituted and who we are. There is no escape from the politics of representation." Stuart Hall, "What is this 'Black' in Popular Culture?" in Gina Dent, Ed. *Black Popular Culture* (Seattle: Bay Press, 1992), pp. 30.
[6]   Freire, *Pedadogy of Hope*, p. 43.

REFERENCES

Freire, P. (1995). *Pedagogy of Hope*. New York: Continuum Publishing.
Henry A. Giroux, Professor
McMaster University
Hamilton, Ontario, Canada

PEGGY RIVAGE-SEUL

11. FAVELA MEMORIES

My first introduction to Paulo Freire was through my reading of the *Pedagogy of the Oppressed*. I had just returned from a year of teaching in southern India, where the exaggeration of wealth and poverty left me questioning my place in the world. Freire's perennially insightful text supplied me with categories for analyzing my economic privilege, as well as my ignorance about which social groups really understand the world. I felt lucky that my graduate school supported my desire to focus my doctoral studies on Freire's philosophy of education.

In the summer of 1982, I attended a two-week course with Paulo at Boston College. He was kind enough to read a chapter of my dissertation, and even declared my work original. I explained my desire to understand what his method looked like on Brazilian ground. Less than a year later, our family of four left on a six-month sojourn to develop our best critical consciousness.

When I wasn't in the *favelas* of São Paulo, I spent my time in the Learning Center arguing with Paulo about the epistemological privilege of the poor. He insisted that the middle class was *fechada* (closed) to the pedagogy of the poor. I was steadfast in my resolve that the middle class was more than capable of understanding class privilege, and wasn't I an example of this?

I lost the argument one day towards the end of my time with Paulo. He had invited me to give a lecture on the subject of my thesis–moral imagination in the thought of Paulo Freire–to his graduate students at Catholic University. After an elaborate explanation of the intersections between Freire's thought, Plato, Immanuel Kant, and Martin Heidegger, Paulo came to the front of the class and thanked me for my eloquent philosophical exposition. Then he pointed to my charts on the wall, and said, "But I don't think you have taken into account the role of the system." I remember the eyes of all his graduate students darting in my direction, watching for my response. I pretended to have difficulty understanding the Portuguese flying around the room. But the truth was that I was shriveling inside from the mortification of my error. After three years of serious intellectual work on the philosophy of Paulo Freire, I had missed his central point. And it all happened in front of the master teacher and his prized graduate students.

After class that day, I returned to Paulo's Learning Center to rewrite the last chapter of my dissertation. I worked night and day to find the missing pieces of my consciousness. Like so many North Americans, I had failed to see the importance of critiquing international capitalism and its accompanying social class structures. On our last night, we were invited to dinner at Paulo and Elza's home so that we could discuss my revisions. Over bourbon and brandy, we read my work aloud. I will never forget his final words to me, "I love this. You have understood."

T. Wilson, P. Park and A. Colón-Muñiz (eds.), Memories of Paulo, 47–48.
© 2010 Sense Publishers. All Rights Reserved.

My time in Brazil was life changing, not only because of the rare privilege to study alongside Paulo Freire himself, but also because I learned to see my own country from the point of view of critically conscious Brazilians. The view from the South was, and continues to be, a painful sight to behold. All the books and economic analysis had not rooted me in a strong understanding of how the world functions for the oppressed majority. It was the realization of my class privilege in the United States, and its accompanying exploitation, that tempted me to stay and work in Brazil. After all, people there, by Freirean definition, lived so much closer to the truth. But Paulo encouraged me to return home to the "belly of the beast" where the real work of the world needs to be addressed.

I returned to Appalachia with renewed vigor. The commitment of Berea College to low-income students provided the perfect classroom to pursue teacher education, in the manner of Paulo Freire. I initiated study programs in Eastern Kentucky where future teachers could see for themselves that the war on poverty was lost in Appalachia. We read *Pedagogy of the Oppressed* so that students would learn to celebrate their cultural capital. After six years of joyous teaching, I received a letter refusing me tenure in the department of education. My best Freirean colleagues, Henry Giroux and Peter McLaren, supported me, but the real strength came from a second lesson that I learned from Paulo. I can hear those words echoing across the lecture hall at Boston College, as if it were yesterday: "Teachers enter their university positions full of critical consciousness about the system. But during the six-year probationary period for tenure, they become domesticated. By the time they receive tenure, the teacher has forgotten his or her promise to change the system." As I sat in my misery and tears, I was consoled by the understanding that I had walked my Freirean talk in the classroom. This time I stood in the spiritual presence of my mentor and had not failed.

In those difficult days, I also remembered a third lesson articulated by Paulo in summer of 1985, again at Boston College: "Teachers must fight for their rights." Crushed by my defeat around tenure, I knew that I had to summon the courage to struggle for relocation at Berea College. The dean's letter had an unusual clause, promising me an alternative appointment because my teaching evaluations were a full standard deviation point above my colleagues. I accepted a part-time position in women's studies. Two years later, I won a Fulbright senior lectureship at the University of Zimbabwe where I offered graduate courses in Freirean philosophy and worked with Africa's finest Freirean grassroots activists. I returned to Berea as a full-time associate professor. Four years later I was awarded tenure in women's studies, followed by full professorship in the spring of 2006. In all these pivotal moments of my professional life, I remained studiously present to the teachings of Paulo Freire. In his words, the painful moments in our professional lives are really opportunities for "making Easter," that is, of letting go of the trappings of prestige and privilege, in favor of struggling for social justice.

Peggy Rivage-Seul
Director of Women's Studies
Berea College, Berea, Kentucky

MANUEL N. GÓMEZ

12. MY MEMORIES OF FIRE WITH PAULO FREIRE

The pedagogy of the oppressed, animated by authentic, humanist (not humani-tarian) generosity, presents itself as a pedagogy of humankind.

(*Pedagogy of the Oppressed*, p. 54)

There is no better business than the sale of fear.

(*Eduardo Galeano, Century of the Wind*, p. 272)

Freedom is acquired by conquest, not by gift.

(*Pedagogy of the Oppressed*, p. 47)

My personal memories of Paulo Freire are almost completely intertwined with my experience of his work and my own goals to implement his liberating pedagogy. I don't know if there is a way to separate out all these different strands, and I don't think it would be in the spirit of what Paulo fought for in his own life and work. Candidly, Paulo has become somewhat of a mystical figure to me, a legend in the way he seemed to promise a way out for everyone like me, everyone who was still living in the paradigm of oppression, trying to escape one end of historical fate without unknowingly fleeing to the other.

I still remember the first time I saw Paulo in person. Although I knew of his work long before I had the means to meet him, by the time I was in a position to have my own work to share and the resources to bring him to the UC Irvine campus and host several dialogues, Paulo was more than a touchstone; the spirit of freedom his work embodied was at the very core of what I wanted to accomplish in higher education for students who had historically been denied access to the social wealth of a university education. I had no idea what to expect, as it was well known that Paulo never approached a lecture or seminar with notes, and he only spoke long enough to open up a provocative dialogue. I waited like a child waits for a new teacher–anxious, excited, hopeful, in awe, really, of what turned out to be a somewhat delicate older man, whose composed presence seemed an unreasonable contrast to his incendiary prose.

It wasn't exactly that Paulo was quiet or shy, but rather that he came to his lectures knowing he had already talked a great deal in his books and papers, wanting instead to listen, to live the pedagogical balance he taught. That those of us who attended him were ourselves perhaps too much like pilgrims on the road to some ultimate salvation could not have escaped his notice, but for our sakes he never tried to jolt us out of our own contradictions, choosing instead to listen

T. Wilson, P. Park and A. Colón-Muñiz (eds.), Memories of Paulo, 49–51.

carefully to everything we said and to hear whatever it was each of us really meant. It was common for Paulo to begin the answer to each question by saying patiently, "What I really hear you asking is ...," intuiting immediately the issue behind the question, offering such a generous empathy that one couldn't help but feel wholly understood and empowered in the dialogue.

Over the years I have thought about how to do justice to Paulo's educational vision, to reconcile the innately revolutionary nature of his work with the inherently slow-to-change realities of higher education. I knew the solution was more in the way of a paradox than an oxymoron; after all, Paulo himself managed to exemplify his own pedagogy, and over the years his work was becoming more and more accepted within the educational mainstream. The combination of fiery passion–the revolutionary summoning of his troops–and empathetic patience was somehow the balance we all needed to achieve, but that was no easy task when so many of us still felt marginalized within our mainstream institutions.

As a Chicano activist, I was energized by Paulo's work at a very visceral level, and I spent a number of my younger years trying to conquer through rhetorical persuasion, protest, and community organizing a space closer to the center of educational opportunities, for Chicano students, and for all students from low-income, minority, non-traditional backgrounds. After all, I had the blood of my Indian ancestors flowing strong in my veins; my very DNA was coded with myriad strategies for resistance and survival. I read Paulo's work along with Eduardo Galeano's *Memory of Fire*, my own imagination sparking from the fire generated by these two visionaries; in fact, so strong was my passion that it burned away any fear of failure or thoughts of compromise. In my youthful idealism, I felt it was past time for the conquered to take back our autonomous power, and I counted on the critical value of education as an agent of social change to host that particular revolution. That the work I shared with other makeshift educational revolutionaries was a threat to the status quo only empowered us. It was, I think, after seeing Paulo in person and engaging in several dialogues with him, that I began to understand that the dialectic process of empowerment was always *mutual*; that is, the true revolution was the uniform transformation of the system as a whole. Cooperation rather than competition was necessary, and fear was the currency of cowards. What needed to be conquered in this particular revolution was not a certain group or leader or class or social position. Instead, the object here was to make everyone a revolutionary by inviting conspiracy on behalf of authentically humanistic values. That was perhaps the most humbling and empowering lesson I learned, and the one that shapes my work most profoundly today.

Simply understanding all this created a revolution in my own heart and mind, because I understood, finally, what Paulo Freire had been about: with his keen mind, patient soul, and generous passion, his revolution was a person-by-person transformational process, the purpose of which was the accumulative change introduced as each mind changed. And it was at this point that I realized that Paulo Freire was wrong about one thing: freedom *can be* a gift, because it's a gift I feel that he gave to me, and the subsequent conquering of my spirit in the service of a pedagogy of liberation has been one which I have hoped to be able to pass on.

Of course I forgive Paulo Freire his mistake in this matter, as his gift did, indeed, give me the tools to conquer some of my own contradictions and self-made obstacles. And after all, it seems completely contrary to all that Paulo represents, to begrudge such a generous gift from such a passionately wise and gifted man.

REFERENCES

Freire, P. (2000). *Pedagogy of the oppressed*. London: Continuum International Press.
Galeano, E., et al. (1998). *Century of the wind*. New York: W. W. Norton & Company.
Galeano, E. (c1985–1988). *Memories of fire* (C. Belfrage, Trans.). New York: Pantheon Books.

Manuel N. Gómez
Vice Chancellor, Student Affairs
University of California, Irvine

RONALD DAVID GLASS

13. MEMORIES OF PAULO FREIRE

In a bathroom; that's where my relationship with Paulo began, in a bathroom at the Center for Latin American Studies at Stanford. I had rushed there, late to a meeting with him that had been arranged by Carlos Torres. Never having been to the Center before, and not being familiar with the Stanford campus, I had gotten a bit lost after the hour-plus drive from Berkeley.

I knew that I wouldn't make it through more than a few minutes of the meeting without first emptying my bladder. As I ran into the bathroom, I was confronted by the evidence of someone making good use of the stall in the corner. After a raucous flush, out steps Paulo, who casually walks up to the sink next to the urinal where I was relieving myself. Introducing myself at that point was out of the question; soon enough Paulo would know with whom he had been sharing this intimate moment.

It was springtime of 1983, and the meeting had come about in place of a cancelled workshop. I directed the San Francisco- and Berkeley-based Adult Education Development (AED) Project, through which I collaborated with a broad range of organizations working on justice, peace, and community issues. I observed at some of their meetings, talked with the members and leaders, and helped analyze their projects to make more strategic interventions in their struggles for justice. The AED Project was grounded in Freire's theory of education as a practice of freedom and in the Highlander idea of democratic education and movement building.

It had emerged from Survival Summer 1980, a nationwide effort by more than 50 peace, justice, labor, and religious organizations to challenge the Reagan campaign for the presidency by raising issues about reducing and eliminating nuclear weapons and power, committing to an anti-intervention foreign policy, and reordering national economic priorities to fund human needs. I had been the Survival Summer organizer training coordinator, and had overseen the development of a resource guide that drew on Freire and Highlander to emphasize the posing of questions to communities and the formation of national strategic commitments rather than the more typical Alinsky-style organizing approach that focused on defining local winnable issues.

The guide, questions, and training structure had been used in regional trainings that prepared more than 750 community organizers for the summer project. The national leadership had built the project base with outreach to organizations in 52 of the largest cities in the US; I had personally traveled to Boston, Cleveland, Minneapolis, Lincoln, Omaha, and Salt Lake City as part of this effort.

T. Wilson, P. Park and A. Colón-Muñiz (eds.), Memories of Paulo, 53–59.
© 2010 Sense Publishers. All Rights Reserved.

In each of these cities, I met with leaders of about twenty local organizations and investigated the themes of their work, the relation of these themes to the proposed work of Survival Summer, and the possibilities for collaborating in the summer project. After the conclusion of the regional trainings that followed the 52-city tour, and after the wind-down of the Survival Summer project, I continued to get numerous requests for more information about our approach to movement building, so I decided to respond to the interest. First, as part my continuing effort to understand the work of organizations struggling to build connections across race, class, gender, and issue lines, I traveled down the West coast–Seattle, Portland, Eugene, Los Angeles, and San Diego–to once again meet with community-based leaders to explore their experiences in this domain and try to discern some lessons from their successes and persistent obstacles. I held conversations of this same type with many groups in the San Francisco Bay area where I lived. I also went to Toronto and spent time visiting a number of popular education organizations and reading through the large collection of Freirean materials at the Ontario Institute for Studies in Education library, making photo copies of as much as I could afford. Out of all these investigations, I founded the AED Project in late 1981. By the spring of 1983, I was working more systematically with about a dozen organizations in Northern California that had a range of foci, including economic justice, anti-nuclear weapons development, identity and race-based cultural politics, or building the learning and political capacities of low-income young adults of color.

When it became public that Paulo had arranged to come to Stanford and participate in some seminars sponsored by the Stanford International Development Education program, word spread rapidly among the AED Project community of activists. The excitement generated was soon dissipated since the seminar cost was beyond a month's income for many–no one elected to pay the fee and instead people hoped to experience Paulo through a public lecture scheduled at the University of San Francisco. Then, several months before Freire's visit was to happen, an opportunity to meet with Paulo arose through John Hurst, a UC Berkeley professor and a longtime supporter of Highlander and popular education in North America. John had been a friend since my Berkeley graduate student days in the mid-to-late 1970s, and he and I owned a property in central Berkeley with two small houses where we lived. John had been invited to sponsor events at UC Berkeley for Paulo, but he thought it would be better to pull together representatives of the AED Project groups so we could spend a day sharing with Paulo the ways our organizations incorporated his theory and getting his critical feedback. We believed that Paulo would welcome that kind of focused time with the staff of grassroots organizations steeped in his conception of liberatory education.

Needless to say, the prospect of this concentrated dialogue was very exciting to all the AED Project collaborators. We began to meet to identify some common themes around which we would organize our day with Paulo. These discussions advanced our understandings of one another and the communities within which we worked, and they built on an existing effort of mine to host small dinner parties to explore barriers to movement building among organizations and activists who often were harshly critical of one another, at least in private. I hoped such intimate settings would permit a deep level of open examination of these criticisms and point the way to building connections on common ground. For example, these conversations could help White middle class feminists learn to reshape their work to incorporate anti-racism struggle, and help some activist young men of color to incorporate anti-sexism struggle into their work; the more that each grasped the perspective of the other, the more hope there would be for building a movement powerful enough to challenge the dominant ideologies of both sexism and racism.

Given all this preparation and the background circumstances, I was shocked to get a call from John a couple of weeks before the meeting with Paulo and learn that we were expected to pay a fee of $2000 to hold the day as planned. This sum was well beyond the capacity of anyone of the organizations to provide–representing several months of operating expenses for some–and even collectively it constituted a very significant amount. Moreover, we were outraged that we should be asked to pay anything at all, given Stanford's comparative wealth. We discussed holding some kind of public forum with Paulo and charging admission or asking for donations, but this idea was nixed because Stanford thought it would compete with other public events already arranged. Without the money, we were stuck.

As I made phone calls informing the group of this unexpected turn, the anger turned to fury; some of the Chicano/Latino young adults vowed to disrupt the lecture at the University of San Francisco by getting there early for front row seats and then standing up to castigate Paulo, in Spanish, for working with the big universities while leaving the community out. Others began to think of other actions that would illuminate the hypocrisy of the universities and their pseudo-embrace of popular education. We wondered how much responsibility should be borne by Paulo himself. I decided to call Carlos to get his perspective, to ask him to pass a letter to Paulo explaining the situation, since it seemed probable to me that he had no idea of what was occurring, and to help us get a one-hour meeting with him. Carlos agreed that Paulo was unaware of the situation, but would want to know about it, and he helped us make contact. Paulo responded positively, and the get-together was set. I brought as many of the participants as possible from the planned day with Paulo, about nine people. And thus the fateful encounter in the bathroom at the Center for Latin American Studies.

I was not many steps behind Paulo when we entered the conference room. Having already met each other as human beings, it was easier to get to know each other as philosophers and radicals. Paulo's eyes were warm and welcoming, though that didn't totally dispel the bit of tension in the room. I thanked Paulo for meeting with us, and then everyone introduced themselves and their organizations. I explained what we had planned for the now-cancelled day, and outlined the themes that had emerged from our preparatory dialogues. Our organizations were grounded in specific communities–Native American, African American, Korean American, Chicano, homeless folks in the San Francisco Tenderloin, lesbian cultural workers, White middle class religious social justice and peace activists–but we had discovered that each of us faced certain frustrations in getting beyond the necessities of responding to immediate needs. It was hard for our organizations to do much more than "keep the patient from dying" and "put band-aids on hemorrhages," although we wanted to heal the community and enable life to flourish. I will always remember my surprise when, after listening and asking a few questions, Paulo turned to me and declared that he was amazed by our projects and that he would come and work with us, for free, whenever I asked. We determined that he would return in a year after we had a chance to make deeper preparations.

In March 1984, Paulo indeed returned. He lived with me and my two children Hannah, 5, and Dan, 3, in my small, 700-foot house in Berkeley for a month. He took over my bedroom, and I slept on the couch. The basic pattern of the month was as follows: he and I would spend one day "hanging out" in the community with one of the AED Project's collaborating organizations, and then one day meeting with the organization's leadership and key members discussing the theme they had identified in the intervening twelve months. In addition, during that month, we held several one-day workshops on general topics: Community Organizing, Popular Education, and Liberation Theology. Each of these had had their own preparatory course of development and emergent specific themes, with about twenty participants drawn from applicants from the "public." We also held a couple of large public "lecture-dialogues," one of which focused on cultural and identity issues that had emerged from the AED Project's ongoing inter-organizational dialogues, and the other of which focused on themes specific to the Native American community.

I have so many memories from that month with Paulo. After long days of work, we would be driving home and, in order to relax, Paulo would sing Portuguese love songs and lullabies. He had a beautiful, soft voice, filled with passion and longing for Brazil, for Elza, his wife, and for his children. Similarly, in the mornings when he awoke, he would talk to me in Portuguese. Of course, it did not matter that I do not understand the language, or that my hearing disability prevented me from learning it. What mattered was Paulo having some space simply to be himself and not always "performing" Paulo Freire. But still, I learned to hear his mood, and enough of the necessary vocabulary to know what he wanted for breakfast. He would laugh and praise me whenever I understood something, and declare earnestly that he could teach me the basics of the language in forty hours if I were willing to subject myself to his tutelage. I would laugh back and ask him where we would find the time in the press of our scheduled work, which had us both worn out at the close of every day. My kids loved Paulo; he was a great person for cuddling with, and he would sometimes read stories to them, each pressed against one of his sides, while I prepared a dinner. Mid-month, the four of us went for a weekend to a beautiful home in Inverness loaned to us so we could get a complete rest. We took long walks at Point Reyes National Seashore; my kids and I would be in our California garb of jeans and shirts, and Paulo in his same daily outfit of slacks, dress shirt, and sport-coat We had long leisurely meals washed down with a well-chosen wine; no one enjoyed good meals more than Paulo. To share a meal with Paulo was to share in an intense pleasure, each moment and taste savored fully. Nothing was rushed, and we talked philosophy and radical politics late into the night. We would recall specific passages or chapters that had inspired our thinking, from Marx, Lukacs, Merleau-Ponty, and Fanon, and discuss the challenges of practicing the philosophy of liberation education. Too theoretical for some, and too practical for others, we had to create our path as we went, without many models and few roadmaps. We laughed about the vagaries of life and the fickleness of fortune, and the powerful role of luck in shaping our identities and our opportunities. We reflected on how odd it was to be the focus of attention, to be expected to be so knowledgeable, when we were so conscious of the limits of our knowledge and our capacities.

Being treated like some guru made Paulo very uncomfortable, but his utter politeness and humility just added to his awkwardness in handling those situations, and so we strategized ways to disrupt the adoring gazes and deferential attitudes directed his way. He never imagined that a veritable Freire industry would arise, domesticating his ideas and work to build market-share. The ironies and contradictions of our lives seemed to know no bounds.

We spent a few days in the central valley of California, focusing on constituent organizations represented in a local group of Christians for Socialism. One of these, Rural Economic Alternatives Project (REAP), was forming producer co-ops among small, mostly organic farms and finding ways to direct-market their goods. In discussions about the nature of co-ops, it was pointed out that one local co-op, Sun-Diamond, was actually a giant corporation, and it had been suppressing efforts to unionize its workers. REAP wanted to penetrate the company to build connections with the workers, so we came up with a plan to get "inside" to do some reconnaissance by posing Paulo as an international agronomist, and Paulo agreed to play along.

We got an appointment for this "important researcher" who wanted to learn more about Sun-Diamond's great success; we took along a "translator," a Brazilian woman who was a University of California student, since we represented Paulo as having very limited English ability. The REAP staff prepared some questions that would be "translated," and we all prepared our roles. When we arrived, we were treated to a multi-media presentation about the Sun-Diamond empire.

When we inquired about how cooperative principles shaped the company, a vice-president proudly claimed that there was "absolutely no difference" between its operations and that of other Fortune 500 companies. The REAP organizer and I would follow up Paulo's prepared inquiries with "innocently naïve" leading questions, and the company representative chattered about their strategies for handling their labor "issues" and for dominating dried fruit and nut production in the valley and globally. Meanwhile, Paulo and our "translator" kept up a satiric running commentary in Portuguese. When we left, we had a long laugh about the success of the ruse, and about how the famous agronomist, who literally had not known the meaning of the word "goat" the day before when it came up in conversation, had overnight miraculously become an expert in California agricultural production. The two hours "inside" provided important grist for the mill in the later discussions about the politics and values of co-ops, and set the stage for a termination of collaboration with one group of farmers whose co-op principles were more in line with Sun-Diamond than REAP.

The final set of memories that I will share concern the work Paulo and I did with the American Indian Movement (AIM) and D-Q University. D-Q was a

Native American developed and controlled two-year college located near Davis, California, that was just recently finally closed down by the federal government after almost thirty years of harassment. During most of the time that I worked with D-Q, Dennis Banks was the chancellor (until he was run out of California under threat of arrest), and AIM's radical commitments animated the campus. Murals told the story of indigenous resistance to European and U.S. conquest, and sweat lodges and annual Sun Dance ceremonies helped maintain the rhythms and sacred connections of community life. D-Q sponsored a forum whose theme was the role of culture in the Native American's resistance to oppression and struggle for liberation. With about four hundred people listening and watching, I moderated the dialogue among Freire and the D-Q scholars and AIM activists. They argued that Paulo's reliance on Marxism and other European thought systems made his theory irrelevant to the indigenous struggle, that its analytic modalities and de-spiritualization of the world was part of the problem and not the solution. They questioned him about whether he was, in a sense, more white than brown, and whether he had sufficiently challenged the dominant ideologies that still inhabited him. The two students on the panel pressed Paulo more directly than the elders, whose narratives posed the issues equally starkly but with less confrontation.

Paulo responded with the quiet force that was typical of him: raising his hands and pulling back his sport coat sleeves, he said: "These are the hands of an intellectual, of a brown man who cannot deny my formation both inside and outside by the culture of the dominant." He defended the value of European intellectual traditions and he also defended the importance of indigenous epistemologies, arguing that the either/or dichotomy undermined a radical grasp of reality. He defended his position as a man of spirit, as a man seeking a way of "becoming a Christian" (not being a Christian), and he again challenged their dichotomous structuring of the issues. The ensuing dialogue was rich with feeling and insight, and drew in more participants from the overflowing room. We ran on well past the established ending time, but finally we had to draw to a close. Rising from the audience, Coyote, a respected elder, masterfully wove the afternoon's conversation into a story and image of a tree that respected the positions of each of the panelists and Paulo, and brought closure to the day. Afterwards, Paulo and I joined a handful of the D-Q spiritual elders in a sweat lodge. Paulo was seated by the entry since he had expressed concern about the stress to his heart and system of the intense heat, and that position enabled the ceremony leader to cool Paulo down from time to time. In the dark heat, each of us took our turn to pray in the language nearest our own heart, and we gave thanks for the opportunity to work together in ways that valued all the relations binding the community and planet together. Later that evening, the conversation of the day continued over a meal of venison and fry bread at David Riesling's home, where we slept. The next day was a gathering of the leadership of all the AED Project-related organizations for an evaluation session looking back on the amazing month with Paulo. We recognized that much remained to be done, but that we were following paths with greater strategic depth, thanks to Paulo's incredible capacity to listen and to help us make sense of our work. That night, Paulo and I were honored at a Native American community dinner, and as we drove home exhausted from intense days, we proudly and humbly wore the necklaces that had been presented to us. These beautiful gifts were more than reminders of the paths we had traveled; they were medicine for our souls as we made the difficult journey toward the distant horizons ahead.

The blessing of my connection with Paulo continues to be such medicine for my soul.

How strange, but perhaps fitting, that we met in a bathroom, in the urgency of our basic human needs.

Ronald D. Glass, Associate Professor
Education Department
University of California, Santa Cruz

PATRICIA GÓMEZ

14. PAULO FREIRE

It was the summer of 1982, when I arrived in California, single parent, three kids; navigating the system to find employment, housing, resources and a support system. Employment came in the form of a teaching assignment which required a four-month training program to implement a bilingual program at an Intermediate school.

Having been a teacher in Mexico, I was told "the students will be the same" by the program coordinators. The group of teachers selected were trained from August until December. The plan was to implement the program in January. We were ready with our materials, and our ideas of how the program would work. I remember the day when I arrived at the classroom. I stood in front of the students expecting them to see me and stand up, greet me and wait for my instructions to start the class, as I had experienced in Mexico. This was not the case. It took me the whole week to calm them down. Later on, I found out that the students were angry to have been placed in my classroom. Their perception was that this was a remedial class. Not only did they resent it, but the selection process the school used to form the class was based on the strangest rationale: the school selected the students based on their Spanish-sounding surnames. In my classroom I had a Filipino student, who did not understand a word of Spanish, kids who had attended school in the U.S. all their lives, recent arrivals, special education students and gang members from opposite gangs. This was 1982.

The rest of the school year was spent establishing discipline procedures and classroom management skills. During the summer, I felt renewed, took reading courses at the University of California, Irvine, established connections with other colleagues and felt ready for a second year. At the beginning of the following school year, I realized that the selection process being applied to form the class-rooms was the same; the students were not essentially different from the year before, and the tug-of-war in the classroom continued. There I was, trying to convince the kids this class was relevant for them, with the students, convincing me, with their behavior, that I was not convincing them.

Needless to say, I left teaching at the end of that year. I felt the kids deserved someone better than me, someone with more experience, someone who could manage the academic as well as the discipline side in the classroom. I felt un-supported and alone.

Upon leaving, I was offered a job working for a non-profit organization whose focus was the prevention of unintended adolescent pregnancy. My responsibility was to extend the program into the Hispanic community.

T. Wilson, P. Park and A. Colón-Muñiz (eds.), Memories of Paulo, 61–62.
© *2010 Sense Publishers. All Rights Reserved.*

During this time, I met Dr. Raul Magaña. Raul had recently arrived from Mexico City, and was working on a research and education project on HIV/AIDS for the Orange County Health Care Agency. He also had a teaching assignment at the University of California at Irvine. We worked together in a couple of educational projects and we became friends. It was through him that I met El Maestro Freire. Raul had invited him to visit California and stay at his house. Raul organized a gathering of friends and colleagues to listen to Maestro Freire. During this meeting, my mind became a film projector. I captured the Maestro's ideas and compared them with my experience as a foreign teacher without the tools to comply with the requirements set forth by the program. As I listened to him, I realized the magnitude of his theories, which by then were considered revolutionary. Time went by, Raul changed jobs, I changed jobs and a few years later, I had the opportunity to travel to Pátzcuaro in Michoacán, Mexico, to attend training for literacy instructors. The Mexican government invited representatives from various cities, each one with different background. Some of us worked at government agencies, others for non-profit organizations, a few were classroom teachers. The training was designed to create literacy modules that could be used in the United States to teach literacy to Spanish-speaking immigrants. The method used was none other than Maestro Freire's, Palabra Generadora. Some of us were familiar with his theories and for others, this experience became a revelation of the profound and yet simple method of teaching others to read and write.

Patricia Gómez
Parent, Family and Community Coordinator
Santa Ana Unified School District, California

MICHAEL W. APPLE

15. AND SOMETIMES WE DISAGREED

After delayed flights, I finally arrived in São Paulo. The word "exhausted" didn't come close to describing how I felt. But a shower and some rest weren't on the agenda. We hadn't seen each other for a while and Paulo was waiting for me to continue our ongoing discussions about what was happening in São Paulo now that he was Secretary of Education there.

It may surprise some people to know that I was not influenced greatly by Paulo, at least not originally. I came out of a radical laborist and anti-racist tradition in the United States that had developed its own critical pedagogic forms and methods of interruption of dominance. I had immense respect for him, however, even before I began going to Brazil in the mid-1980s to work with teachers' unions. Perhaps it was the fact that my roots were in a different but still very similar set of radical traditions that made our public discussions so vibrant and, certainly for me, compelling.

There were some areas where he and I disagreed. Indeed, I can remember the look of surprise on people's faces during one of our public dialogues when I supportively yet critically challenged some of his positions. And I can all too vividly remember the time when I had just gotten off those delayed flights and he and I quickly went to our scheduled joint seminar before a large group that had been waiting for us to arrive. The group was made up of the militants and progressive educators he had brought to work with him at the Ministry of Education offices in São Paulo. During the joint seminar, I worried out loud about some of the tactics that were being used to convince teachers to follow some of the Ministry policies. While I agreed with the Ministry's agenda and was a very strong supporter of Paulo's nearly Herculean efforts, I said that–as a former president of a teachers' union and as someone who had worked with teachers in Brazil for a number of years–there was a risk that the tactics being employed could backfire. He looked directly at me and said that he and I clearly disagreed about this.

The audience was silent, waiting–for distress, for "point scoring," for a break in our friendship? Instead what happened was one of the most detailed and intense discussions I have ever had in my life. For nearly three hours, we ranged over an entire terrain: theories about epistemologies; the realities of teachers' lives; the realities of life in *favelas*; the politics of race and gender that needed to be dealt with seriously alongside class; the international and Brazilian economy; rightist media attacks on critical education in Brazil and on him personally; what strategies were needed to interrupt dominance in the society and in the daily lives of schools; his criticisms of my criticisms of their strategies; my suggestions for better tactics; and the list could go on and on.

T. Wilson, P. Park and A. Colón-Muñiz (eds.), Memories of Paulo, 63–64.

This wasn't a performance in masculinities, as so many public debates are. This was something that demonstrated to me once again why I respected him so much. There was no sense of "winning" or "losing" here. He was fully engaged, wanting to think publicly, enjoying both the richness of our dialogue and our willingness (stimulated constantly by him) to enter into a field that required that we bring in *all* that we knew and believed. For him, and for me, education required the best of our intellectual and emotional resources. I'm not certain we ultimately resolved our disagreements. I know that I was taken with his passion and his willingness to listen carefully to my worries–worries based on my previous experiences with political/ educational mobilization in other nations.

I also know that he took these issues very seriously (see, e.g., Apple 1999). Perhaps a measure of this can be seen when, after that three-hour dialogue that seemed to go by in a flash, he had to leave for another meeting that had been delayed because of our discussion. As he and I said our goodbyes, he asked the audience to stay. He then asked me if I could stay for as long as it took so that the audience and I could continue the discussion at a more practical level. What could be done to deal with the concerns I had? Were there ways in which the people from the ministry and from the communities that were in the audience might lessen the risk of alienating teachers and some community members? What strategies might be used to create alliances over larger issues, even when there might be some disagreements over specific tactics and policies?

It is a measure of Paulo's ability as a leader and as a model of how critical dialogue could go on, that another two hours went by with truly honest and serious discussion that led to creative solutions to a number of problems that were raised as people reflected on their experiences in *favelas* and in the ministry. This to me is the mark of a truly great teacher. Even when he wasn't there, his emphasis on honestly confronting the realities we faced, on carefully listening, on using one's lived experiences to think critically about that reality and how it might be changed– all of this remained a powerful presence.

This was not the only time Paulo and I engaged with each other. We had a number of such discussions in front of large audiences. Indeed, in preparation for writing this brief remembrance, I took out the tape of one of our public interactions and listened to it. It reminded me that what I've said here can't quite convey the personal presence and humility he had. Nor can it convey how he brought out the best in me and others. One of the markers of greatness is how one deals with disagreement. And here, once again, Paulo demonstrated how special he was, thus giving us one more reason that Paulo–friend, teacher, comrade–is still missed.

REFERENCES

Apple, M. W. (1999). *Power, meaning, and identity*. New York: Peter Lang.

Michael W. Apple, Professor
School of Education
University of Wisconsin, Madison

TOM WILSON

16. MEMORIES OF PAULO

A Plethora of Encounters

My memories of Paulo, drawing from my encounters of 27 years with him, are of
two parts. The first calls to mind his initial thirteen-year influence upon me through
his written work. The second captures his impact as I came to come to know him
personally for some fourteen years.

PART I

In 1969 I became an Assistant Principal for Curriculum and Organizational Development at Newport Harbor High School (NHHS) in Newport Beach, California. As
I best recall, my first introduction to Paulo's work was through his Harvard Educational Review seminal article Education for Critical Consciousness. I was hooked
to say the least. I then became hooked squared when I read *Pedagogy of the Oppressed* shortly after its initial 1970 publication in English. I immediately began to
explore his work with those teachers who I believed were interested in critical
pedagogy in relationship to their own classroom situations. In the fall of 1978, while
still an administrator at NHHS, I supported the teachers in a labor dispute. When
ordered by the principal to give to him the names of the faculty who I knew to be
involved in a threatened work slowdown, I asked him what would be done with the
names. He replied that those teachers so identified would be subject to disciplinary
action with notation placed in their personnel files. I refused to carry out his order on
ethical grounds. Next I found myself meeting with the deputy superintendent where
I reiterated my stand. At essentially the same time the teachers called off the slowdown so no names were required, yet I informed the principal and the district
administration that if the teachers decided to move ahead at some future time,
I would not obey. To my surprise, there seemed to be no further moves by either the
principal or the district administration although the relationships between us remained
strained to say the least. However, in March 1979, the last legal day for official
notification, the principal handed me a letter from the superintendent stating that my
services as an administrator would no longer be required for the coming and subsequent years and that I was to be reassigned as a teacher somewhere in the district.[1]
   This was the first time I had any inkling that things were amiss, for in the five
months since my refusal, there had not been a single indication of the district's
intentions. I immediately filed a grievance with the support of the district school
level administrators organization against the principal and the superintendent.
As I worked my way through this entire struggle, I found firm ground to say

T. Wilson, P. Park and A. Colón-Muñiz (eds.), Memories of Paulo, 65–69.

nothing of solace, in returning again and again to my developing knowledge of the lessons offered by Paulo. Winning the grievance seemed to be less and less important and I soon came to understand that, as he was wont to say, "in the final analysis" it was time for me to move on.

I spent the next year (1978–79) at Loyola Marymount University Los Angeles (LMU) as the Director of the Student Development Center (SDC) housed within the university's Student Services administrative unit. I was attracted initially by the Student Services finely written, articulated mission for Social Justice and subsequently impressed by the language I heard in the interview process. Thinking back to my NHHS experience, here was a marvelous chance to apply my understanding of Paulo's philosophy and practice to the ongoing functioning of the SDC, to "concretize" (a Paulo favorite) the notion of student democratization and liberation within a post secondary education context.

I saw this forthcoming LMU experience as an opportunity to deepen my understanding of Paulo in the real world. And this did happen through many conversations with young Jesuits versed in liberation theology with particular reference to their struggles in Central America as well as working with a number of undergraduates deeply committed to progressive cultural change through university and community based social action projects. However, and retrospectively from my perspective, as I became more embedded in the university, the mission for social justice often seemed to be not matched with corresponding just action within the confines of the Student Affairs Office and as it turned out more importantly, university senior administrators. While there were a number of conflicts between the SDC and the university at large, of particular note was the struggle by students (lead by students working in the SDC and supported openly by the SDC) to establish a gay/lesbian/transgendered student organization, a move strongly resisted and eventually, officially not permitted by the Catholic university senior administration.

As the academic year 1979 came to a close, once again I was informed that I would not be coming back to LMU since there seemed to be incompatible differences between my beliefs and those of university and that the SDC was to be refigured. No hard feelings of course! Aha, an epiphany, the liberation game indeed is risky and here I am looking for a job once again, thank you, Paulo.

In 1980, I took a position as Director of Instructional Development (IDS) at the University of California Irvine (UCI). In 1983 Richard Regosin, Professor of French, and I received a major three-year grant from the National Endowment for the Humanities (NEH) designed to engage secondary teachers in the study of ethics, aesthetics, and critical reasoning and their application to classroom practice. As part of this grant, I was able to make contact with Paulo through the efforts of Peter Park, then at the University of Massachusetts, Amherst.[2] This was the first of many encounters with Paulo. Without exception, all meetings were for me close encounters of the best kind saturated with the I-Thou relationship of which Martin Buber writes. Rather than list a chronology of events, I want to offer a number of events that for the most part illustrate his humor. For me, they provide some of my warmest memories. While these descriptions are random and not in all cases exact words spoken, hopefully they do capture the moment, the essence of the encounter.

PART II

On a Saturday in the mid 1980s, we are at Santa Ana Community College in Santa Ana, California. The city of Santa Ana is about 92% Latino/a with Spanish as the first language. It is a full day gathering of students, parents, educators, and community members. Paulo begins his talk by asking if he should speak in English or Spanish. Not surprisingly, the answer comes back "Español." He then requests a translator to accommodate the English speakers in attendance. The translator is one Feland Meadows, associated with a local school district as a bilingual and early childhood specialist. Paulo suggests that he will speak just enough to enable Feland to keep up and that it is OK to interrupt him if he is going too fast or if Feland needs clarification. Feland returns with his own OK. Paulo begins with Feland taking notes. After what seems to be an inordinate amount of time, Paulo stops and asks how Feland is doing. Feland replies he is doing fine. Paulo then continues with Feland note-taking in concert. Paulo once again pauses and says something to the effect that perhaps Feland might now be ready to translate. As Feland proceeds, a look of joyful surprise spreads across Paulo's face as he exclaimed in wonderment "this is amazing, it is fantastic, he said it better than I did!"[3]

On another occasion in casual conversation, Paulo cited a time when he began a talk to a largely bilingual English and French group by asking if French or English would be appropriate. French was the general response. So he began. After a few moments, he was interrupted by a member of the audience who politely who said, "Paulo, if you don't mind, would you switch to English?"

In the early 1980s, Paulo's first visits the University of California, Irvine. My administrative assistants Terri Egan (then a MBA student, and now Associate Professor of Organizational Behavior at Pepperdine University, Los Angeles) and Sheila Kenny invite Paulo for lunch at Zócalos, a Mexican restaurant, across the street from the University. After a lengthy and satisfying meal, Terri and Sheila state it would be their honor to pay for the lunch. Paulo would have none of it; he picks up the check and informs them, "I can afford to buy lunch, I make enough money on *Pedagogy of the Oppressed.*"

On the many occasions that I heard Paulo speak, either in small dialogues or large lectures, he often used the expression "in the final analysis." I have forgotten just where I raised the question that if we really believed in the final analysis, would not such a belief be a contradiction because there no longer could be a further analysis thus shutting down the dialectic. He looked at me for a moment, smiled, and then responded, "yes, in the final analysis Tom, I think you are correct."

We are in a relatively large lecture hall once again at UCI. Paulo has been invited to address a gathering of some 50 or so math and science teachers attending a workshop whose exact purpose escapes me, except it was not centered on either Paulo's work or critical pedagogy. When asked by the convener prior to his talk, how many were familiar with or had even heard of him, I recall no one responding. I think Paulo, sensing this lack of knowledge began by asking if anyone had a question. Initial silence was followed by more silence until finally a question was posed. Paulo then, as I have observed him to do many times, just "took off," analyzing the question from this point of view, from that angle, circling it, contracting, honing in, then nailing it, from my perspective a beautiful response. However, the questioner did not see it the same way: "I am confused, you didn't answer my question." Paulo remained quiet for just a moment, and then softly said, "Well, I thought I had."

Standing in front of two elevators in the Administration building at UCI, Paulo notices that the one on the left is open with an "Out of Order" sign posted. He starts to laugh. I ask what is it that he finds so funny. He replied that in Brazil there would be no sign and that people would go into the open elevator and just wait until something happened.

Paulo is meeting with Myles Horton at Loyola Marymount University Los Angeles in the suburb of Westchester to give a series of workshops as well as to put the finishing touches on their book, *We Make the World by Walking*. After the last meeting and as the sun sets, about ten or so of us begin to organize ourselves to drive from Westchester to a home in Pacific Palisades for a party in honor of Myles's 82nd birthday. Somehow after everyone has seated in several cars, Paulo and I remain on the curb. I suggest that we take my 15-year-old Camaro, a vehicle that he had admired several times after previous rides. He agreed and off we went after receiving verbal instructions from the party host. Pacific Palisades, sitting above the Pacific Ocean, is a tangled mess of illogically arranged and light-deprived streets. As we engaged in serious discussion, increasingly I become aware that I am completely lost with Paulo Freire by my side. I do know that if I can backtrack to Sunset Blvd and head west, we will end at the ocean on Pacific Coast Highway where I could call the host for new directions (obviously, this memory pre-dates cell phones and GPS). As we pull into a gas station and find a phone, I offer a confession and apologize profusely. I make the call, get back into the car, and once again express my guilt. Paulo turns to me, places his hand gently on my shoulder and says "Do not worry, Tom, I have been in many worse situations than this."

In this last memory, Paulo was only indirectly involved. Often I find it curious by the number of individuals who I would expect to know of him but do not, as well as surprised by those who I would expect not to know him, but in actuality do. In 1992, I retired from the University of California to take a position as the Director of the Master of Arts in Education in the School of Education, Chapman University, Orange, California. I had asked Paulo if he would be willing to write a letter of recommendation for me and he readily agreed. On my first day at Chapman, the Dean of the University Faculty warmly welcomed me. After a very amenable discussion, as we shook hands at the end of the meeting, she smiled and said to me, "We are so glad you have agreed to join us, Dr. Freire." Now, dear Paulo, in memory, what was I to do with that?

NOTES

[1] Within the school district, administrators cannot have tenure as administrators but after three years of satisfactory service they have earned teacher tenure regardless of having actually taught or not.

[2] For a description of my first meeting with Paulo and several other memorable encounters, see Wilson, T. (2008). Learning moments: Raging a bit, and with hope. In S. Nieto, *Dear Paulo: Letters from those who dare teach* (pp. 67–70). Boulder & London: Paradigm.

[3] Feland Meadows is currently the Goizueta Endowed Chair of Early Childhood Education at Kennnesaw State University, Kennesaw, Georgia.

Tom Wilson
Director, Paulo Freire Democratic Project
College of Educational Studies, Chapman University, California

ANAIDA COLON-MUÑIZ

17. UNFORGETTABLE ENCOUNTERS

How does one person change our lives so powerfully? I am in awe of Paulo Freire and the impact he has had in my life and that of so many other educators. My memory is clearly marked by him. From my earliest experience in teaching, I was moved to change my view of literacy and the world by his words in *Pedagogy of the Oppressed*–my eyes were made wide open. As a beginning teacher in New York City, I knew that my charge was to follow his calling for a greater *conscientização* and to view and practice education as a process of liberation for me and my students. I viewed the world from a new perspective from then on and saw the realities of how schooling had become a source of domination instead of freedom. I knew I could make a difference by the kind of teacher I could become.

BANK STREET TEACHER CORPS STUDY GROUP, NYC

As a Teacher Corps student at Bank Street College of Education in 1974–1975 in New York City we didn't study Paulo in the master's degree program, but rather a group of us formed our own study group and began meeting outside of our teacher education classes, reading his work and putting it into practice in the schools where we were placed as interns. We began to practice our teaching based on this critical view, challenging the status quo/debilitating teaching that was typically practiced in many public schools We started creating curriculum based on generative word, as we understood it. I was in a 3rd and 4th bilingual class in District 3 or Morningside, on the upper west side of Manhattan. I remember we used words like *cheque* and *ropa* to work with students for whom the monthly check that arrived was critical for them to get clothing and other things they needed. One of the teacher interns began developing large silk screen posters of workers-pictures that depicted the actual lives of the families in our community and not the false lives of those in the books printed for our schools–those books of White families with stay-at-home moms vacuuming and cooking in puffy dresses and dads who arrived at 6 pm for a family dinner dressed in black suits and carrying leather briefcases–those "Leave It to Beaver" families were not our reality, and promoting those images in schools through books and the media only served to perpetuate a false consciousness in our students that could hinder, rather than help them. Paulo inspired us to use the students' lives and experiences as beginning text and their voices as literature.

PRAXIS, NEW YORK CITY AND AMHERST, MASSACHUSETTS

Our students were bright and excited about learning and inspired to work on actualizing their lives. Through our work, our school's neighborhood became the classroom.

T. Wilson, P. Park and A. Colón-Muñiz (eds.), Memories of Paulo, 71–75.
© 2010 Sense Publishers. All Rights Reserved.

With studies on Nuestro Barrio and Our Central Park Science World, we spent time in our community walking it, studying it and understanding it as the reality that was, and the possibilities of what could be. The art of teaching was changed forever, as we engaged in a praxis for literacy and liberation that was rooted in the realities of the lives of our students as Paulo taught us, and not in the packaged curriculum that appeared in our books. Paulo's shadow was always with me as a young teacher, but up to this point, I had not met him face to face. Even during my doctoral studies at the University of Massachusetts in Amherst, his writings permeated the work we undertook with Dr. Sonia Nieto and Dr. Luis Fuentes. I gave birth to my son Marco in 1980, right around the time that Paulo came to at UMASS as a visiting scholar, and I remember a gathering at Sonia Nieto's house where everyone surrounded him like a celebrity. At that point our encounter was but a brief glance and recognition of each other's presence. I smiled in awe of him, he nodded. But, his presence in Amherst was greatly felt by all of us and he, once again, left us his legacy to do good, critical work in our communities.

FINALLY...IN CALIFORNIA

After completing my coursework, I left Massachusetts for California in 1982 with my family. I finally had the chance to meet Paulo at several meetings. During one of his presentations at University of California, Irvine probably around 1983, I was thrilled to sit in the same room with him and watch him challenge a young student who had asked Paulo to define *Critical Pedagogy*. Paulo retorted by asking the student to define it as he understood each of these words. He asked him what the word "critical" meant to him, and then proceeded to ask him to define "pedagogy." I will never forget the look on that student's face as he struggled to define these words, with Paulo's prodding and help, of course. He made each of us think deeply about the meaning of words and titles, and to not take anything for granted, because there is deep meaning in words that reflect our world, and how we view it and live in it. I recently moved and found my notes from that meeting. They were carefully written in a small UMASS notebook, front and back pages. I was thrilled to read my interpretation of his powerful words and wisdom. One of the things I wrote were statements he made on *knowing*, which helped me to view this word through a new lens. Reflecting deeply on the construction of knowledge is critical for educators, yet is typically relegated to what is contained in textbooks and tests. According to my notes, Paulo said that, ... *"because of repression and discrimination, which the majority of minority cultures suffer, they make knowledge while suffering, with knowledge of their limitations."* (UCI, 1983). He also said that,

> Knowing is about the subject and object–avoid misunderstanding the dialectic– which is not mechanistic–but rather our whole body is into the process. The need to know should be optimized– knowing how to know–[this is] not a neutral act–[but] political (in favor or against something)–for example, being in favor of a dream or ideal and against those who don't favor it.

That same day, I happened to enter the elevator with Paulo–another close encounter indeed. I took advantage that we were alone and we spoke briefly about bilingual education, a major concern of mine. We spoke about it as if we were old friends. Then, he said something that perplexed me at first, and it wasn't until much later that I understood what he meant. In so many words, he said that if the United States' policies and practices were not so racist against people of diverse language and racial backgrounds, we probably would not need bilingual education as we knew it. Confused, at first, I thought that perhaps he was not in favor of bilingual education. Later, I understood what he was saying–that we must have bilingual education because of our struggle for the rights of the children to be accepted for who they are and for their possibility to become protagonists of their own lives. Bilingual education is a necessary act and struggle created by conditions of the powers that be in the United States vis-à-vis those who are subjected to its oppressive stance with regard to language, culture, race and power. It took me a while, but it became clear to me, and that clarity has helped me to view not only bilingual education as a political act, but other areas in education as well.

THROUGHOUT MY LIFE

Some years later I returned to Massachusetts in 1989, thrilled to watch Paulo receive an honorary doctoral degree alongside my husband Mac Morante, who was completing his doctoral degree at UMASS that same year. These were so many close encounters. I was not a close friend, however, he had changed my life as an educator and his presence seemed to be with me, and this gave me comfort and strength.

Thus, when I was given the charge to co-coordinate the conference for the California Association for Bilingual Education (CABE) in 1991 in Anaheim, I never imagined that I would have another life-changing Freire encounter; one that again would serve as a model for us, not only because of his words, but because of his action.

My dream was to have Paulo give the opening keynote speech at our bilingual education conference in California which had over 12,000 attendees at the time. Without first checking with the CABE board, Mario Castaneda (who was CABE staff at the time), my colleague, Silvina Rubenstein, and I decided to try to make this happen, and we so began planning. My job was to try to make the contact and arrangements. I had been transformed as an educator by Paulo's teachings, and now was our opportunity to have him touch the lives of thousands of other teachers in California who worked with bilingual students.

I did the only thing I could think of at the time, and it was to call him at home. I can't recall exactly how I got his number, but I called.... and he answered the phone! Our conversation was brief, but in my Spanish, English and limited Portuguese, and his Portuguese, Spanish and English, we were able to communicate well and he agreed to be the keynote speaker. I nearly fainted with joy and disbelief! I was totally enthralled by the idea of having Paulo at CABE and we began our promotion for the program and to make the necessary arrangements for his travel. Once others learned that he would be in California, we began to get requests to have him present at UCI and other venues. They wanted to take advantage that he was in the States and have him present to other audiences. Unbeknownst to me at the time, one of the individuals interested in having Paulo visit was Tom Wilson, Paulo's dear friend and now my colleague at Chapman University and my collaborator in this book.

Then, the Gulf War known as Desert Storm began. Papa George Bush and a coalition of countries decided to enter Iraq and the bombing began. We were all horrified by this war and its sensationalism through the media, where the bombing and killing was promoted as if it were fireworks at a local amusement park–so much so that some people called it Star Wars. But, we all knew it represented devastation and death for many civilians in those cities we were attacking. It then came as no surprise when I got Paulo's call that he could not put his foot on the soil of such an aggressor nation as the United States. He cancelled his trip. My heart sank, our plans to have Paulo present were shattered, but I fully understood why he was not coming. He explained that he would come at another time when our country was not at war, and that he would help me to find someone to speak in his place for the conference. He selected another dear friend of his, and now my colleague also in this text, Peter Park. It seems as if he was weaving the web of critical pedagogues who would continue his work internationally long after he was gone, although he would never propose such an effort.

Peter Park appeared on that day of the California Association for Bilingual Education Convention in 1991, It was held in Anaheim at the Convention Center. The room was overflowing at the opening session. Peter was introduced by Alma Flor Ada; two of Paulo's dear "discípulos." Their words rang in the room of over 4,000 and Paulo's spirit came through loud and clear. I will never forget Peter's actions, as he took his written speech and refused to read it. Instead, he proceeded to talk about his own journey in recapturing his life as a Korean American whose language and culture had been usurped by America's need to promote a scholar. He spent the rest of the time, denouncing the US involvement in Iraq. A few of the leaders of CABE looked at me in shock, as some members of the audience got up and left. "Anaida, what is going on?" the board members asked. "It's okay," I said. I thought to myself, "This needs to happen. He has to tell the truth as Paulo would expect him to expose the insanity of the war." It was not until the following year that the CABE participants would be able to hear Paulo's words directly from his lips, as he kept his promise to come to CABE once the war was over. At this point, the noted event has remained one of the highlights of CABE history.

But, that fateful year, in 1991, when Paulo refused to enter the United States, he made his stance clear–his sense of justice, and his strong principles were a lesson for all of us who might get so caught up in the planning of a convention that the true mission gets clouded. Bilingual education and critical pedagogy can not be separated because the powers that attempt to control knowledge still don't get it. We are still here, finding ways to make that critical difference. More than 10 years have passed since Paulo left us, but I think his presence and his words are stronger than ever in the work that we do in education. It is also more than 10 years since Proposition 227 showed its ugly political face to unveil the contempt that there was for bilingual education and our students and teachers. Paulo helped us to understand that we must stand by our beliefs no matter what the politics are or the price we have to pay.

Thank you, Paulo, for your guidance, your teaching and your presence. My encounters with you and your words have truly been unforgettable.

Anaida Colon-Muñiz, Associate Professor
College of Educational Studies
Chapman University, California

IRA SHOR

18. "THE GENERAL IS ARRESTED!"

On a cold winter night in February 1984, I was driving alone to Amherst, Massachusetts, en route to dinner with Paulo Freire. News came over the car radio about the arrest of General Galtieri in Argentina, the recent head of that nation's military junta, now disgraced for losing the Falklands War to Britain. Hearing the report, I was happy that a junta somewhere was crumbling, and thought back to the most important political event in Paulo's life: the 1964 military coup in Brazil. Twenty years earlier, a junta had destroyed Paulo's literacy project along with social movements then in progress. Paulo was jailed and then forcibly exiled; others were beaten, some tortured, others killed. The April coup in Brazil erupted just as Paulo planned to open 20,000 new "culture circles" nationwide. This and other cultural action for freedom was too much for the generals and the wealthy elite they served. We can only imagine what might have been accomplished had those thousands of culture circles opened, had Paulo lived his most productive years in a democratizing Brazil. After the coup, Paulo's books were banned in Brazil as was Paulo himself, perhaps the most Brazilian person you could meet, hopelessly in love with the language, food, drink, dance, and music of his homeland. With his body and imagination cut off from the culture that created him, Paulo's "pedagogy of the oppressed" went underground at home and abroad with him.

Unlike Argentina, where Galtieri was arrested, the Brazilian generals were never held accountable for the repression launched in April, 1964. Their iron rule and economic failures provoked popular resistance which finally forced a "democratic opening" through which Paulo and his family could return in 1980. Two decades after the momentous coup that changed his life, and four years after returning to Brazil as a man of sixty, Paulo was still on the road, now in Amherst as a famous world educator in constant demand, honored with awards from the U.N., with doctorates from universities, and with a monumental sculpture in Scandinavia. His *Pedagogy of the Oppressed* was being read in many languages, his public meetings filled beyond capacity.

Years of patient work and militant politics by him and others enabled recovery from the violence of the April coup. Still, ruptures like 1964 derange history, deforming the life of the nation and Paulo's life, too. Consider that Paulo was removed from his native country in the prime of his oppositional work. An emergent national movement for democracy was decapitated. Until that April morning, the language and conditions of Brazil fed Paulo's radical imagination, a concreteness that no other space or place could offer in his many years of world travel ("a peregrine of revolution" and "a vagabond of the obvious," he sometimes humorously

T. Wilson, P. Park and A. Colón-Muñiz (eds.), Memories of Paulo, 77–79.
© *2010 Sense Publishers. All Rights Reserved.*

said about himself). That winter in Amherst in 1984, he spoke to packed auditoriums and eager seminars in a language foreign to him, hoping that his presence might be a "pretext" for local opposition to gather, coalesce, and advance.

Happily, I was coming to dinner with some good news in my pocket–A *general* was actually in jail, not a literacy educator! I met up with Paulo in the elegant living room of a university dean. I barely finished conveying the news of Galtieri's arrest when Paulo sprang off the sofa with such elation that I, too, stood up and so did our hosts. When Paulo noticed we were all standing with him around a coffee table, he registered some embarrassment, explaining how important it is to hold generals accountable for violence. This incident was an unexpected education for me in the pain Paulo carried for Brazil, for himself, and for other countries that suffered coups in the dreadful decades before and after 1964, when the CIA was busy around the world.

Paulo's open passions endeared him to many, as did the unusual accessibility of this famous man. He was approachable and unaffected; he spoke plainly and did not want to be worshiped. Of course, he was passionate about social justice, which gave him authority in representing "the pedagogy of the oppressed." It was his passion for justice that sprang him to his feet when hearing that the general had been arrested. A week after Galtieri's arrest, I was in Paulo's Amherst apartment, when that passion leaped out of him again. Earlier that day, we had shopped in a supermarket for pasta, vegetables, and good vanilla ice cream (Elza's favorite, he told me as he put it in the cart). Later, after dinner, Elza went to sleep early, and Paulo and I washed the dishes, then watched a late movie on TV, which happened to be "Judgment at Nuremberg," the well-known depiction of Nazi leaders on trial after World War II. I had seen the film before when it came out in the U.S. about the time of the coup in Brazil. As the story unfolded on TV, Paulo became more and more involved with the action, as if the trial were happening live in front of us. He again said how important it was to hold the military and the government accountable for their crimes, something not done in Brazil. (The message stays with me: While we were in Amherst, the Reagan Administration was illegally financing the murderous Contra War against Nicaragua; in 2003, the second Bush Administration notoriously lied about WMDs in Iraq to start that horrendous war there.)

Perhaps, after all, we can say that Paulo used well his survival of the 1964 coup. He lived and worked as if he were accountable to those who had been killed, tortured, jailed, driven underground, and left behind. In long exile from the culture of his roots, he wrote key books and encouraged a global audience to question the unequal status quo in the name of social justice. But, as Paulo himself said, opposition can change a society only when situated in the concrete limits and possibilities of the places where resistance takes action. As an involuntary exile, forced out of Brazilian history just when it seemed on the verge of democratic changes, Paulo made the best of his wandering life abroad, growing a beard to keep warm in the North, learning to speak publicly in a language hard for him—English— sharing conviviality with activists at meals, nudging along forces of resistance when he could. What he could not find abroad was the concreteness of Brazil, the place and space that created him and which his radical labors sought to transform.

Social justice was to him a dream made real by recreating history with your own hands, as he liked to put it. When news of General Galtieri's arrest sprang him to his feet like a young athlete, not a man of 63. He spoke eloquently with his body, telling us that fine furniture in a living room is nice, that world travel and fame have their rewards, that good food and drink in the company of friends is a blessing, that romantic love is delicious, but that a world of social justice counts more than anything else we can receive, achieve, or imagine.

Ira Shor, Professor
City University of NY Graduate Center and
The College of Staten Island, CUNY

TERRI EGAN

19. THREE DISTINCT MEMORIES OF PAULO

My memories of Paulo are of three distinct periods. The first is when he came to Irvine for a series of summer dialogues in the early 80's. The second period is after his wife Elza's death when he seemed lost and quite fragile. The third was after his remarriage to Nita. Each encounter was markedly different and, as I reflect, has left an indelible mark on my own practice as an educator and organization development practitioner.

As a 23 year-old single mother working at the University of California, Irvine pursuing a Masters Degree in Business Administration as a means to support my young daughter, I lived in a world of contrasts and contradictions. In my courses I studied how to manage people and increase profits.

My part-time job on campus in Instructional Development Services working for Tom Wilson exposed me to theories and practices related to transformative change and organization development. I also had the opportunity to meet a number of people who were involved in the critical pedagogy movement.

The first time I met Paulo was in the mid-1980s at UCI where he was in residence for a series of dialogues. Educators and community leaders came from all over the U.S. and stayed on campus. Part of my job that summer was to make sure that Paulo got to where he needed to go, and was generally taken care of.

The first day I met him we set off on the Los Angeles freeway system in my aging VW bug for an interview at a public radio station. My sense of direction being poor—and my interest in talking to Paulo great—it was a surprise that we made it to the station at all. Needless to say, we were late for the interview. Rather than being angry, Paulo was kind and expressed appreciation to me for driving.

Later in the week, I observed some of the dialogues. It was the first time I had witnessed large group discussions with people convening around important topics. Such a diversity of people and perspectives led to an emotionally charged environment which ultimately generated a deeper understanding of the issues. Watching him with the group, I was struck by his presence and the impact of his questions.

That summer was punctuated with the joy of spending time with Paulo and those in the local community—many of them Brazilians—who were his colleagues and students. At the end of his visit someone gave me a copy of *Pedagogy of the Oppressed*, and he signed it for me and thanked me for being his friend. Long before I understood his philosophy I was captivated by his warmth and generosity. I wanted to understand more about the teachings of this man that I connected to at an emotional level.

When I next saw Paulo I was shocked to see how frail he appeared. He was depressed over the loss of his wife Elza. Accompanied by his daughters, he came

T. Wilson, P. Park and A. Colón-Muñiz (eds.), Memories of Paulo, 81–83.

to Southern California for a conference in her memory. In addition to helping with the conference, someone suggested it might be nice if I took Paulo to Disneyland. He seemed fascinated by the park. As we walked through the various lands he repeatedly exclaimed, "incredible." He loved the Small World ride, became quite disoriented on the Circle Vision panoramic movie about America, and was troubled by the lack of diversity in the characters in the Main Street parade.

That evening we went to a local restaurant where my daughter Brook serenaded him with a song in Japanese that she had learned in preschool. He was charmed by this living example of the small world and thought it was wonderful that she was learning about different language and cultures. To this day she remembers how warmly he treated her.

The day at Disneyland with Paulo and his adult daughters stands out for me as the first time I walked on familiar ground, in a place that I took for granted as positive, and saw it through the eyes of someone with a vastly different perspective. My critical eye was awakened at Disneyland with Paulo Freire.

The last time I saw Paulo was at a party for him and Nita. To my delight he appeared happy and healthy. He sat with a group around him talking about the transformative power of love–how everything in his life had become sweeter, more vibrant. It strikes me now how the image of him full of joy in the relationship was a deep testimony to the power of love and our essential ability to recover from grief and trauma.

Ten years after meeting Paulo I was a young assistant professor teaching a required Business Ethics course to MBA students at the University of Southern California. I had come to view my task as converting the heathen capitalists to a more enlightened view. The back of the case room was typically filled with the most cynical and unwilling students. Boredom, crossed arms, and the occasional snide comments greeted my lectures.

One day the topic was affirmative action. A question from the back: "Why do we have to have a club for all of these groups, women, minorities, gays? I don't see any clubs for White males." My answer, "Interesting question, some might say that the entire University is one big club for white males." I saw the pain in his face and knew at that moment I had humiliated him and lost any chance, at least in the short run, for him to hear me or value the subject. I was embarrassed, and apologized.

Later that evening I recognized that my growing resentment of the students was leading me to climb up on my soap box and lecture more stridently for each class. I remembered the story of Paulo as a young educator admonishing a group for using corporal punishment with their children. A man in the back of the room challenged him to understand the experience of those parents before passing judgment.

I knew that I had been judging my students without understanding their perspective, and had contributed to creating a classroom environment that was adversarial rather than transformational. The clarity that I gained from that experience has profoundly shaped me as an educator and practitioner.

More than twenty years have passed since I first met Paulo. In the classes that I teach in organizational behavior, critical thinking and organizational development I introduce my students to his work.

My hope is that they are also introduced in some small way by my practice and how I teach as much as what I teach. By the extent to which I live out my belief in the power of hopeful and restless inquiry, the importance of integrating emotion, reason, intuition and spirituality, and the inherent resilience of human beings when they are motivated by love and a passion for justice.

Terri D. Egan, Associate Professor
Applied Behavioral Science
Graziado School of Business Management
Pepperdine University, California

BROOK LARIOS

20. AGE IS NOT RELEVANT

Racism, bigotry and other mentalities of inequality are enough to scald the thickest of skins, but often overlooked are the effects of ageism. I have become acutely aware of this as I continue to grow in my profession as not only a woman, but one who looks younger than my age.

I was a child when I met Paulo Freire during his work with the faculty at the University of California, Irvine. At the time, I was too young to comprehend his philosophies and the extent of his work, but I will always remember his warmth and compassion. Paulo never treated me as a child or subordinate, but rather as a human being. I understood, even at a young age, that he respected me and valued me as an individual. He presented himself with an aura of joy and humility in every encounter. His name made me smile.

Growing up, I spent an extensive amount of time around adults and enjoyed conversing with my distinguished counterparts. Because I was accustomed to mingling with adults, I grew embarrassed and resentful when I was treated as a child or made to feel small. Teachers sometimes did this. I recall standing up to my fourth grade teacher when he ridiculed me and the surprise on his face. I knew, early on, that I would not settle for inequality due to my age and that I would not believe in the caste system that the education establishment had created, with the professor or teacher ranked as top dog.

My encounter with my fourth grade teacher was only the beginning of my challenge with the social constructs of education–a challenge that Paulo had met head-on. I found myself once more questioning the role of education during my freshman year of college. It was the first day of a required humanities class and my professor asked us to reveal our expectations for the semester. I said that I expected that the instructor would not allow his opinions to dominate the dialogue so that we could think freely and craft our own ideas about what we were learning. Now, with an understanding of Paulo's philosophies, I estimate that his influence on my family may have helped shape my ideals.

When Paulo's colleagues at the University of California, Irvine set up a trip to Disneyland, he insisted to my mother that I come along. That meant the world to a child who looked up to her mother and colleagues for their intelligence and creativity–a child who was eager to become an adult. Additionally, I recall attending a party at Paulo's home, where I was first introduced to Brazilian food; I had never seen black beans before. Even though I grew up in a melting pot of other cultures and my parents ensured I was exposed to a variety of cuisines, it is possible that this encounter drew me even closer to the idea that our differences should not be

T. Wilson, P. Park and A. Colón-Muñiz (eds.), Memories of Paulo, 85–86.

dismissed, but cherished. I remember the kindness his wife and daughter showed me and the happiness that swirled through the room as we celebrated life together.

Now, as a writer and public relations professional, I look back at the world in which I was raised and I see traces of Paulo's light in my philosophies. My mother, Terri Egan, who was profoundly impacted by Paulo's friendship, is no doubt one of the vessels for these beliefs. I am confident that every person I encounter can teach me something. I believe in active, not passive, education. I believe in social justice and I root for the underdog. And, I know that if I were able to spend time with Paulo today, I would experience his wisdom in a whole new way. How blessed I am to have spent time with him in person and to experience his wisdom and grace still.

Brook Larios
PlainClarity Communications
California

CESAR ROSSATTO

21. FREIRE'S PEACEFUL REVOLUTION

And a Word for Those that "Sell Out"

Dear Paulo, I have fond memories of you and your influence on many of us under-going the daunting times of military dictatorship in Brazil (in the 60's to the 80's); your contribution offered us a way out. My first encounter with your work changed my life forever and in a very deep way. I was studying with Nita Freire and other great professors at a local university in São Paulo, when your theories first hit me. It was a turning point in my life. I learned that "to be neutral is a political position," one more in line with a conservative notion that maintained oppressive systems.

At that time I was in the seminary studying to be priest and trying to be politically neutral, until I studied that all of us are political beings. I realized that by avoiding the development of critical consciousness, or by ignoring and silencing oppressive political outrage, I was the status quo accomplice. It also goes without saying that guilt was very familiar to me at that time. Since I was living and working with people in their worst poverty conditions, I learned very quickly that I had to stand up for what I believe in and be committed to social justice and change for democracy. I found my real "vocation" as an educator and gave up the seminary to follow grassroots movements. For that I am very grateful to you.

If I had the chance to talk and dialogue with you again, I would tell you that your life example and social commitment made a major difference in my life. I am changed forever. My life is much more meaningful. It had been worth every bit of the way.

As you would say, "a true revolution comes out of love–a deep sense of commit-ment to others, where oppression is abolished to restore the love which that situation made impossible." Paulo, we need to remember this and all aspects of your life and contribution, since I have seen many taming your legacy and only remembering your take on banking education. They forget the whole idea of social transformation–just like some mention Martin Luther King, by bringing up the "I Have a Dream," speech and forgetting the whole movement, its struggle, and important principles you built on for us. For others, your name also became a commercialized symbol, lacking feelings and commitment. We certainly would hope to keep your teachings alive as the basis of this and other struggles needed today. As you had said, in response to Tom Wilson, when he asked if you had developed fully critical consciousness, "I am working on it." I understand that critical consciousness never reaches a stage of perfection or at least a stagnated plateau but it is a constant process of new and evolving discoveries.

Nevertheless, one can also deny it, and "sell out." I remember attending one of your classes at PUC (Potificia Universidade Católica–Catholic University) in

T. Wilson, P. Park and A. Colón-Muñiz (eds.), Memories of Paulo, 87–90.
© *2010 Sense Publishers. All Rights Reserved.*

São Paulo, Brazil, where you made a critique to Cardoso, the Brazilian presidential candidate at the time. I remember you saying that "he sold his soul to the devil" for abandoning and betraying his principles to the socialist commitments. Ever since he allied himself with the most oppressive extreme right wing politicians of Brazil, who tortured people in the 60's, in order to rob the election and defeat his opponent Lula. Lula was a strong leftist union leader, from the Workers' Party who had only 6th grade of formal education. Lula became president after Cardoso. If I had the chance to talk to you again, I'd say that your support to the Workers' Party paid off. I really admired your sense of integrity to the cause, and for not showing any mercy to people who "sell out," even though, in contrast you also knew how to express kindness and respect for conservatives who didn't know any better.

People circulate on internet this anecdotal as an oral tale created by you Paulo. It really gives a good illustration of your position about different kinds of knowledge. The tale goes like this:

THE BOATMAN

On a long flowing river, difficult to cross,
There was a boatman who helped
people to cross from one side of the river to the other in his boat.
On one of those trips,
he was transporting a lawyer and a teacher.
Being someone who talks a lot,
 the lawyer asked the boatman:
Do you know about laws?
No, responded the boatman.
"You've wasted half your life," responded the
lawyer feeling pity for the boatman.
As equally social the teacher joined the conversation
 and said: But you know how to read or write?
Again, I do not, replied the boatman!
How pitiful! You've wasted
most of your life! Said the teacher
At that moment a strong wave hit the boat and capsized it sending all three into the waters.
Worried the boatman inquired:
Do both of you know how to swim?
No! They quickly answered, going down the stream.
What a shame, replied the boatman
Both of you are losing ALL of your life.
To Freire inference: "There is no superior or inferior knowledge.
Just different kinds of knowledge."

It is funny and it also gives away a good lesson. I like it in particular because it values non-formal kinds of knowledge. Most amazing, for instance, is to have Lula as the president of Brazil besides his limited formal education and yet he proved to be more effective and popular than other president in Brazil. You were right, Paulo, an organic leader who is able to develop wisdom from his/her praxis and collective engagement can be just as knowledgeable and efficient as anyone else or even better.

Paulo, your name and your work became a metaphor–a role model symbol among others we admired and held in high regards, so for us you will always remain alive. Paulo, I remember what you told me when I interviewed you in your home before I turned on my recording, you said: "don't ask me any question about armed guerrilla revolution, Fidel Castro… any of that." To my response "why," you answered, "because it brings a lot of pain and suffering to both sides–both lose," indicating to me that your ideas of a revolution or social change had to be through peaceful means. Your interview clarified it more deeply, explaining that "social transformation happened if people were able to develop critical consciousness, regain their humanity, and learn to live with each other."

Reflecting back in our encounters and dis-encounters, I realized that these kind of small details are not small when we look at the big picture and understand the meaning of your philosophy. These details are insights that reveal greater aspects of your life, work, and legacy, which for me are treasures and sources of wisdom gained directly from you, one of my greatest "gurus." I don't mean to idealize you, since for me you were very human; but you were one of the biggest influences in my intellectual development. For me, it was in your sense of humility where your wisdom emerged so naturally. What amazed me the most was your humble attitude. I visited your home and learned that you kept all your awards hidden in your bedroom. That proved to me that you didn't have to be a show off, like many in academia who become prima donnas, pushing to "make a name," and be famous. I admired seeing your home full of symbols of popular culture, with religious statues, sensual figures, and books all over; signifying to me aspects of someone who loved life and therefore were able to embrace people with their life's struggles and creeds.

Paulo, we no longer have to read your books secretly any longer! Like *Pedagogy of the Oppressed* during those days of military dictatorship, that systematically prohibited the readings of your books. It was hard. We now can read freely your work. Thanks to your presence in this world and contribution, we have come a long way more recently. We had grown in terms of new understanding and leftist movements for the betterment of life and justice–in particular feminist, racial, critical pedagogy, and environmental awareness, theories, and movements. In regards to social democrat political movements, Latin America, for instance, had made major advancements; you would love to see that. We have many new leftist governments, including women as elected officials. Many countries are picking up a real positive vibe and a real sense of hope. In contrast, in the U.S. we had gone backwards, under the Bush administration, by expanding the neo-liberal ideology agenda, imposing the detrimental standardized testing systems in the public schools–NCLB, and crime against humanity through unjustified wars. As a consequence, poverty and oppression in the U.S. and some other countries around world is growing. On the other hand, in the U.S. there are some new promises in the horizons with new administration.[1]

Further along, unfortunately, even the liberation theology movement also had a setback with the new pope. Thus, Paulo, I would say after all the strides forward we made in the world since *Pedagogy of the Oppressed*, we also need "Pedagogy of the Oppressor," especially for those born in more privileged countries, which have a hard time understanding hegemonic and oppressive systems within "developed countries like the U.S., because they are part of it. Above all, we need an in-depth understanding and intellectual development to deconstruct whiteness or white supremacy and patriarchy, together with elitist capitalism.

At last, I am glad you reminded us that "people that are afraid of critique risk becoming dogmatic." I agree we have to be critical even of ourselves. Nevertheless, I also know that some critiques especially from people on the left can be at times too harsh, as you had experienced and commented how painful it became for you in some instances. Now I know what you mean, since I also experienced it. The worse can be those critiques from comrades who at times can be cruel. So, Paulo, I would say that critique needs to have at least common sense.

I also will never forget the day I came to your home for the interview when you asked me about that U.S. school principal who punished a kindergarten boy because the toddler had hugged his classmate and kissed her. The principal accused the boy of "sexual harassment." I will never forget your disdain to this insanity and shared your outrage. Your critique was called for and necessary. Your pedagogical ideas make a lot of sense to me–on one hand to denounce and on the other, to announce. I understand that being critical of everything unjust is a natural approach to those committed to social justice. The lessons learned from you became part of my existence and participation in this world.

One thing that amazed me the most from your existence in this planet, was the fact that you were able to use and transform your personal experiences of struggle to better understand other peoples' struggle and be able to better help them, just like you did with your literacy experiences. You learned to read and write pretty much on your own as you couldn't go to elementary school, but later you used that personal experience to understand and assist adults on how to read and write. That for me is the most fascinating and memorable insight I have about you. Thank you!

I also remember crying when I read the news that on your way to the hospital, you asked the nurses "not to let you die, because you wanted to see the turn of the century..." and the hospital's report saying that "your heart was the size of a child's heart..." I knew that your desire for life and your ability to love were the finest. You set the example until the last minute. I recognize then that your whole life, your last words, and even your own body were witnesses to the fact that you practiced what you preached, even to the very end. Your example will be remembered, I am forever grateful to you, thanks Paulo.

NOTES

[1] This was written before the historic presidential election of 2008 when Barack Obama was elected president.

César Augusto Rossatto, Associate Professor
The University of Texas at El Paso

HERBERT J. BERNSTEIN

22. FREIRE, SCIENTIST

The idea that hope alone will transform the world, and action undertaken in that kind of naïveté, is an excellent route to hopelessness, pessimism, and fatalism. But the attempt to do without hope, in the struggle to improve the world, as if that struggle could be reduced to calculated acts alone, or a purely scientific approach, is a frivolous illusion. *Pedagogy of Hope*, Paulo Freire.

INTRODUCTION

Almost every day I see a smiling, slightly faded Polaroid of the graying Paulo Freire. Not a shrine, not a framed icon, the photo just happens to be out in the messy dresser-top muddle where everything, current and not-so-current alike, mixes together at the beginning of my day. The SX-70 camera that took it came from a Kellogg Foundation grant in 1984, to document the people who helped me learn. I was the scientist seeking humanities and ethics training, not for self-improvement nor simply to perfect my interactions with society, but to know what I was taking on–and to finish a book on causes and effects of modern knowledge. It is called *New Ways of Knowing*.

Always there, on my dresser, the photo never fails to give me pleasure. In the photo Paulo is happy. It is Myles Horton's eighty-second birthday party at a house in Pacific Palisades. They have come together in California and, with the help of Sue Thrasher, on staff at the Highlander Center, are "talking a book" on education and social change: *We Make the Road by Walking*. I shot a short video of Paulo on that occasion, where he says, comparing himself to the towering Horton, "I am just an underdeveloped man from an underdeveloped country." The video also records his definitive comment about nature and culture:

There *is* nature. It is not only a mere construct; and it *includes* the human beings who are part of it. But the moment a human looks at nature, there is no longer nature alone. It is nature as seen through culture.

NATURE, SCIENCE AND CULTURE

Here Paulo was challenging a distinction–nature *vs.* culture–often drawn by those who privilege sciences above other human endeavors. And in modern society most of us tend to privilege the sciences as the fount of reliable knowledge. A prevailing understanding of scientific practice entails belief in its methodological objectivity, progressive directionality, and emotional vacancy. But virtually everything about this understanding is wrong or exaggerated.

T. Wilson, P. Park and A. Colón-Muñiz (eds.), Memories of Paulo, 91–100.

Paulo's remark at the birthday party shows the sophistication of a reflective scientist, one who knows that the usual categories are at best only partially true of modern sciences. In my own work I try to recognize, even utilize, the muddle that replaces such dichotomies as nature-culture, pure-applied, use-misuse, even science-technology. When one is more completely open to the complexities of modern knowledge, everything changes: everything from who you work with, to what problems you choose, to how you write up what you have investigated. To do the necessary reconstruction of sciences my colleagues and I worked on theory in *New Ways of Knowing,* modified our procedures, changed and supplemented our work, and eventually founded the ISIS Institute for Science & Interdisciplinary Studies. It became a new house of experiment–pursuing its initial projects in both physical and biological science on two continents–to try out reconstructive science "in the field." The Institute recently passed the fifteenth anniversary of its incorporation; a record of ISIS efforts can be found on the website http://isis.hampshire.edu. Paulo's work was an inspiration to our own.

PAULO'S EFFECT AND CONNECTION TO NEW WAYS OF KNOWING

Paulo was not just a model of a new thinker/doer, as reconstructor of the science and practice of popular education. He was also the source of several ideas for work in the sciences. He inspired me and my colleagues not merely in teaching sciences to empower the students, but in challenging framing assumptions too, also by modeling the characteristics of a different kind of science. Although Paulo worked in education, his focus recognized the preeminence of personal/political development; reconstructive science recognizes that dimension in technical scientific work, too. So ISIS emphasizes dialogue, empathy, self-awareness and critical inquiry. This is in many ways the opposite of the "prevailing understanding" of sciences, cited above. As scientists who see themselves serving a larger social purpose, see important historical constraints to their craft, and read their own fields' publications not only as the latest best revealed Truth, we need to proceed differently. We must recognize cyclic processes in sciences' development: the dustbin of history contains insights to future "discoveries." And self-awareness calls for critical inquiry: what are the unasked questions? And who are the unrepresented classes or groups of people?

If the ultimate justification of current knowledge is "It Works!"–as is the case in my own field of quantum mechanics (and in many other fields of highly technical post-modern work)–you must go on to ask "Works for whom?" "And works to do what exactly?" At ISIS we are constantly asking these questions, of ourselves, our fields, our projects. From cleanup of the military environmental waste that years of legal exemption and improper procedure have amassed, to inquiry into the future of a world shaped by genomics, to pioneering indigenous aquaculture in the Ecuadorian Amazon region, we seek ways to reunite with inquiry, often quite close to Freirean inquiry, in order to make knowledge–or remake it, actually–and to understand it in a new way.

But let's back up a bit here, and put the story chronologically. We'll follow my encounters with Paulo first in theory, then in person, and finally in sadness; returning to the present and recent past for a conclusion.

ENCOUNTERS

Theory and Practice

I recall first hearing about Freire in a seminar with Marc Raskin, Susan Buck-Morss, Ann Wilcox and Joe Turner at the Institute for Policy Studies in Washington DC, all of whom participated in making the first *New Ways of Knowing* volume. We were grasping at ways to reconstruct modern knowledge and especially the sciences at its head. All of us hoped to show that excesses, seeming side effects, and untoward consequences of modern knowledge were part of its misconstruction. We sought examples where combining politics (and the values of empathy, human dignity, deep social justice) into the framing assumptions and basic processes of a field would make a big difference–a difference which would keep the results of inquiry consonant with the loving intention that scientists often bring in by way of our motivation.

Eventually, perhaps, new definitions and practices might spare some of the contradictions we now live with–situations where we, as researchers, end up serving interests and values far from our own–and even farther from the youthful enthusiasms and interests that attracted us to our particular fields in the first place.[1] As a physicist, I think of the so-called inevitable link between energy and environmental damage, on the one hand, and destructive military might, on the other. Physical science seems unable to sever such linkage anywhere in the coal-petroleum-nuclear triumvirate of energy sources; why had solar, wind or renewable energies never become a mature technology like these three? Why did the best and brightest science always seem to serve the richest folks and basest instincts?

We were Excited to Learn about Freire's Work

Paulo started from where the "students" were by introducing materials intimately related to their daily circumstances and struggles with unjust power. Topics and readings in Freirean education are quite vital to a student's own interest and yet somehow, if the "teacher" is skilled in these techniques, globally significant.[2] It was an approach so clearly infused with both value and politics that it did not engender contradictions; it rather used them to further the educational ends. Perhaps there was a method here that has inherently good–such close contact with necessary values, such an intricate dependence on political awareness, that it could never succumb to the fallacy of use/misuse. Use/misuse arguments always follow analysis that would say "knowledge is power; and power can be used for good or evil." Instead of serving with power wherever it led, here was a knowledge practice requiring the correct politics, good values, straight analysis. It could never get effect for the wrong ends, it starts and finishes without the values that make those errors occur.

No sooner had we decided that Freire represented a leading edge of knowledge reconstruction, than we learned an important lesson. His was a in great field for such a lead development, that of *alfabetização*–literacy education. It would be entirely fitting for the scientists and knowledge workers to adopt as a method that which was pioneered to help a quite different class of people struggle against the system. We saw Freire's approach as a method whose very basis in radical politics meant it could not be used in an anti-human or illiberal way. The lesson came from an unexpected source.

The New York Times ran an article within weeks of our discussing merits of Paulo's work, which generated delight at finding a great way of combining knowledge with critical political insight. The article was about the Con Ed Company turning to Freirean techniques for training immigrants and unskilled workers to repair modern electrical distribution centers. The trainees were not illiterates; and they certainly were not being taught with materials based on raising their class consciousness. Clearly the City's corporate monopoly supplier of electricity was not interested *alfabetização*. At least one of the company's goals was to tap a low wage labor pool.

This reminded us that reconstructing knowledge requires deep consideration. An approach that magically avoided all the ills of twentieth century knowledge, avoided all the consequences of two centuries of the rise of power under dominant economic systems, would need more sophisticated analysis and subtler practice. It could not depend only on the adaptation of a simple "technique," no matter how successful or attractive in its field. The path to reconstructive knowledge is a process, not a thing. It needs more than a simple search among existing practices, a minor job performed like collecting coins or picking up progressive hints from here and there around the globe. Even the application of Freirean techniques would need to be explored by doing.

Meeting Paulo in Person

Several years later I met Paulo in person for the first time in a wonderful weekly seminar series that ran one month each year for several years. Paulo had a "gig" at the University of Massachusetts' School of Education which brought him and his wife Elza to the Valley. I was fortunate enough to be invited as a member of the Five-College faculty. I joined ten others to form the seminar with Paulo while he visited Amherst. Everyone was excited; delighted, honored, to be in Peter Park's "Education, Values, and Human Action" faculty seminar; all of us wanted to ask our own questions, to work directly with Paulo, in effect to become his students.

To be honest, we were a motley crew. Though I was probably the only "hard" science researcher, overall we drew from disciplines as diverse as sociology, communications, psychology and physics. We tended to speak past, around, over and under one another. The ideas were not all from lefties or leftist perspectives. Someone often played the devil's advocate for capitalistic and for individualistic, almost anti-socialist, values. We had straightforward pragmatists, strong socialists, a couple of hermeneutical and critical theory buffs and several Marxists, to say nothing of the discourse analysts; all of us contributed. But Paulo seemed to transcend these differences, to speak to each of us, and to listen to each of us with deep respect and concentration.

In our seminar, Paulo talked about the concept of "conscientization" (i.e. *conscientização* in Portuguese) as a melding of both consciousness raising and developing one's conscience. Perhaps his ideas on the etymology and purpose of the word had been recorded elsewhere, or perhaps not even until today, but the point he made was then quite important to us. It was an eye-opening opening remark for the four week seminar. Here is a segment from the still unpublished raw transcript of our discussions:

> Paulo: Let us consider the word *conscientization*. First of all, this word is *conscientização* in the Brazilian language. In English you have 'conscience' and 'consciousness,' and these words have different meanings. In Portuguese we have different meanings but we understand the meaning in the context. For instance, we can say in Portuguese '*Pedro e um homem de consciência*,' 'Peter is a man of conscience.' We are then using conscience in the moral meaning. If, however, you say '*a consciência humana capta o concreto*,' it means 'human consciousness grasps the concrete.' So the word *conscientização* comes from 'conscience' in Portuguese. Before, in the 1960s, when this word conscientization, *conscientização*, began to come up in French, English and Spanish, and became the catchword of many liberals, the word was very much attached to me, associated with my writings. Because of that, people thought I had been the father, the creator of this word. Historically, this is not true! I did not invent the word. As of now, in Brazil we are not sure about the real source of the word...

That unpublication of our transcript is a story in itself to which I return below: suffice it to say that members of the seminar were quite divided over whether, how, and in what form to publish, or even to transcribe the work. I was among a minority who believed that an indication of the dialogic process was helpful–certainly not publishing all the hem's and uh's and stumbling repeats, but some present indication (whether by font or attribute, notation or notes) that all of us as academics had edited our words to make them sound more smooth. That might have made the transcript more interesting to those who hadn't attended–nearly an honest record of conversation, of mutual inquiry with shades of deferential disagreement mixed into the eager (but unfamiliar) role of student in which we all, junior and senior professors alike, willingly placed ourselves.

Paulo always started from where the student left off. He would repeat the last statement you had made, "Yes, Herb! The actions of science are predicated on thought..." or "Oh, yes, Mary. The question of giving someone a moment of clarity..." and go on to completely instruct (sometimes even instructing the opposite position from the one enunciated or implied by the student's statement) as if it were the most obvious and correct next step to take–as if, in fact, the student were clearly on her or his own path to that very insight already, without any help from the teacher.

This is a great method to use on almost anyone, but especially those who feel abashed, embarrassed or afraid to be seen not knowing something already. And, certainly, we have all felt this way, and learned more and appreciated learning more for this kind of gentle guidance. His qualities of humility, generosity, curiosity, hopefulness and honesty, not to mention humor, were as much a part of his work with us in person as they are a part of his writing. So often one finds that heroes turn out to be rather ordinary and self-absorbed when you actually meet them. Paulo was the man, the teacher, that he appeared to be in his work and more.

One year I finally had the courage to invite Paulo to the *Classé Café* in downtown Amherst to talk about my reconstructive scientific project under the rubric of "Science, Understanding, and Action"–a variant of the seminar title that starts from the assumption that values are already built into the sciences. One cannot separate what Paulo Freire said from the way in which he said it. But what he said about science made me feel that Paulo was genuinely interested in the sciences. He seemed to view them as I did, though he was not invested in creating hard science himself. And the gentle humanity, the full attention that Paulo brought was clearly felt by my young daughter. Carrie had such a good time with us over a bagel and a cup of coffee that she remembered him, the *Café*, and the occasion of that meeting quite well; it may come to her again from time to time now as she enters a graduate program for policy studies.

Why was I in that Seminar?

My students and former students had told me that I'd always "naturally" and unassumingly put my politics into all my technical and applied work. It came into my teaching as a matter of course: I believed that asides, colloquialisms, introducing the themes and sweep of a critical history were necessary to learn the physics without accepting its cover story. Apparently, I mixed these value-laden ingredients into even my theoretical work, my research. And they all knew it.

The sciences are important places to get a thoroughly political and unillusioned form of consciousness embedded in the pedagogy–and perhaps into their content, too. Ceding power by adopting a "value free" stance only means letting in the values of those who can fund the research that *they* wish to see successful. Eventually it means the scientists cede even the definition of their own fields. Concerns of taste and discrimination–judgments, in short–always define what we consider to be good science, and who we believe are the best and smartest scientists. The rich and powerful are smart, too. They know their own interests, pursuing them into science itself.

This was the heart of the matter for me. I thought the Freirean approach to science education would inform the eventual content of sciences, as well as their discovery process. That larger task was what I hoped to learn how to do–not just to teach in the Freirean way, but to improve the future science I would do and, more importantly, all that my students would produce.

Paulo's incredible style and world-class technique as a teacher did not disappoint. I was used to other collaborators' rather direct "Yes and," delivered with a good, seemingly sympathetic and very smart repetition of the last thing someone said. But they would always go on with a statement or issue of their own, whereas Paulo would seem fully interested in what you'd said. And he would genuinely be interested. Your thoughts provided an opening. It was an occasion to learn and to teach. It seems to me that difference is what we need today: the ability to take you to greater consciousness and conscience, led there by the answers to his well-chosen questions coming out of your own mouth.

Seeing Paulo in Brazil

In the same program that led to *New Ways of Knowing*, our group of Kellogg Fellows went to Ecuador to learn about international issues. I had proposed an additional activity, piggybacking on our presence in Latin America–an additional trip that I expected to help me work more closely with Paulo. Among other things, the two of us were to be involved with Peter Park in writing a book, based on the U Mass School of Education conversations. I wanted to see for myself the working conditions for Freire, and the possibilities to collaborate with him at a distance: how hard was it to teach in Campinas, so far from São Paulo? What were the facilities and utilities at Freire's disposal?

The mechanism for our trip was additional funding from Kellogg. The Foundation had decided that if several Fellows joined forces in a learning activity, a short proposal might merit a supplementary grant to their fellowships. I proposed visiting Paulo Freire and several action/education organizations in Brazil. In short order six Fellows signed up and we received our grant. A Kellogg staff member helped us get in touch with an interesting guide, someone who worked with popular education for at-risk women in Rio de Janeiro. I added a couple of scientific stops, including a physics institute in São Paulo that was doing science-for-the-people outreach as well as modern experimental physics and an appointment with the chancellor of Campinas University, a prominent Chicago-trained mathematician who was pioneering in ethnomathematics.

These were all fascinating stops–and they each reflected the vitality of Paulo's, and others', initiatives for forms of popular education in Brazil. But disaster struck, even while we were out of our country in Ecuador.

Suddenly and unexpectedly, Paulo's first wife and lifelong companion, Elza Maia Costa de Oliveira, died without warning the week before we arrived in São Paulo. We saw him very briefly right outside a memorial service for Elza and were left with only the surrounding activities, the few days in Rio and the memorable two-hour trip to Campinas. My mission to see his circumstances was successful but the increased ties for collaboration did not materialize.

Paulo never returned to his Amherst visiting schedule: those trips, that seminar, the University were too closely linked to life with Elza, her loss too present in his mind. The book on our Five-College "conversations on sciences, education and social action" was fated never to be published!

Paulo's trips to the USA, usually during our winter, relocated themselves to southern California where that photo on my dresser was taken. I still have transcripts of the seminars, accompanied by ancient computer diskettes. So does Peter Park. His efforts to gather a few salient questions from the original seminar participants succeeded, and several of us prepared at least the start of our answers. But we never retrieved Paulo's draft answers and remarks about the questions. They were lost somewhere between Brazil and his longtime translator here in the States. And the work can no longer be completed.

CONCLUSION

Finally, I'd like to consider a couple of events after Paulo's death. They lead back from working with him to teaching in the Five Colleges. One happened while preparing the first education course *per se* that I'd ever given at Hampshire College. Oddly enough, this was just fall 2007. It was a senior seminar, modified from what I have usually taught under the rubric of *New Ways of Knowing* by accommodating itself to recent changes in the college's curriculum. I was scheduled to teach a select group of advanced seventh semester students how to mentor an independent study, one mentee per student. We needed a few books as the intellectual core to pull the group together.

I thought that something of Paulo's about teaching teachers to foster their pupils' independence would work, but when it turned out that only two class members had read *Pedagogy of the Oppressed*, that classic became the obvious choice. I quickly found that the first English edition had a gendered-language problem which was solved in the twentieth anniversary reissue (and, of course, the thirtieth), so we read the later translation. My Freirean position of teacher-learner in that class came to the fore quite strongly. I learned about senior seminars, about the oppression inherent in assigning summarizing tasks as part of personal reaction papers, and a great deal about how to let go of a student-initiated, peer-to-peer assisted learning program. This seems like another step in the process of my work with Paulo, bringing it back to education and sciences.

In a sense, that course constituted follow-up to several such efforts over the years. One highlight was the summer 2005 "Liberative pedagogies" conference of Professor Donna Riley at Smith College who teaches in their new undergraduate Engineering Program. Though Donna is too young to have been in the Five College seminar with Paulo, her whole career bespeaks his influence. She has gone much farther in her teaching than the asides and broad commentary in my physics and seminar classes; her basic engineering thermodynamics course raises issues of purpose, social choice and decision-making quite explicitly. The influences which historians of science have known for years, and which leftists like Boris Hessen and J.D. Bernal connected to modern applications, are finally making their way, through explicitly liberation-oriented education, into engineering curricula: a field I least expected to ever embrace Freire.

In short, the synthesis of Freire's ideas within sciences and technology seems to be happening.

Sciences

The impossibly effective revolutionary enterprises which I have contended must be most concerned to keep learning, keep changing, by staying close to questions. Paulo Freire, renowned for his dialogic methods in teaching, was certainly close to questions in the sense of using them extensively. But elsewhere (*cf. Muddling Through*) we have seen that staying close to questions by not assuming definite answers, not buying too closely into one's own assumptions, not seeking answers at the expense of finding yet further new questions–these are the signs of a twenty-first century scientist at work. In this regard, Freire was a scientist and science spreader of the highest order.

Freire

Paulo Freire more than anyone had the way of staying close to questions, using questions to get at the answers, questioning the assumptions we all overlook, helping whole classes to question the assumptions of society. Paulo was the not just the master teacher, he was a model of the reconstructive scientist as well.

EPILOGUE

I'd like to thank my students who taught me the importance of education as a field, especially the MIS kids–Karl Campbell whose extraordinarily graceful expression in philosophy of science has informed my work and is incorporated in some phrases of this piece; Mary Bridon-Miller co-authored an earlier article that informs part of this work. Sue Morse from whom I first learned the value for reconstructive science of education; Aryenish Birdie getting excited about the use of animal as a pejorative, a distinct negative–where Paulo complained in Chapter 4 of *Pedagogy* about having that term applied to working people, even in the version retranslated to a modern ear for eliminating sexist language. Is the trend for liberation and inclusiveness continuing? What would an attempt look like to make the same point (the evil inherent in degradation and dehumanization of the non-patrón campesino) without slipping into anti-animal denigration of his own; my feeling is Paulo was not a sexist when his gendered language identified the self-fulfilled and fully human characters as male, that perhaps he is saying it is wrong to call the poor "animals" in the same way it is wrong to denigrate their Macho. Perhaps the more complete expression (as in the newest translation w.r.t. women) is to uphold both poor people AND animals. Clearly the invisible speaker in chapter four, the oppressor, is denigrating both in his verbal move –just as he was to men and women in the earlier translation of chapters 1–3.

Thanks to my amazing co-authors Marc Raskin & Mike Fortun for their writing suggestions at various stages and to my wife & daughters for reading the draft versions.

NOTES

[1] Situations like the one two fine biology students from the first *New Ways of Knowing* class faced several years ago. They thought biology (="study of life" after all) would embody the love of life and all its forms which motivated them to major in it. But in their first professional work, at Yale in

a summer research project, they found out they had to "sacrifice" thousands of hapless creatures for each footnote their boss accumulated towards his next paper. I never viewed the anti-vivisectionist position as relevant to real science until they espoused something very close to it as a result of direct experience.

[2] Quotation marks around "students" and "teacher" reflect Freire's recognition of the great learning achieved by dialogical teachers and how much the students teach them and learn, translated into the terms teacher/learner and student/teacher.

REFERENCES

Fortun, M., & Bernstein, H. J. (1998). *Muddling through: Pursuing science and truths for the 21st century.* Berkeley, CA: Counterpoint Press. See also its review: Physics World 13, 47, (March 2000). Electronic version. Retrieved from http://physicsworld.com/cws/article/print/2443.

Freire, P.. (2000). *Pedagogy of the oppressed* (30th anniversary ed.). London: Continuum International Publishing Group.

Freire, Paulo (2000). *Pedagogy of the oppressed.* New York: Continuum.

Horton M., Friere P., Bell, B., Gaventa, J., & Peters, J. (Eds.). (1990). *We make the road by walking: Conversations on education and social change.* Philadelphia: Temple University Press.

Raskin, M., Bernstein, H. J., Buck-Morss, S., Chomsky, N., Goldhaber, M., et al. (2006). *New ways of knowing: Science, society and reconstructive knowledge,* corrected large format version (2006). CBLS, Marietta OH. First published by Rowman & Littlefield (1987).

Herbert J Bernstein, Professor of Physics
ISIS Institute for Science and Interdisciplinary Studies
Hampshire College, Amherst, Massachusetts

RUDOLFO CHÁVEZ CHÁVEZ

23. I REMEMBER PAULO...

In my eulogy to Paulo, one of many from a diverse community of scholars, published in a *Taboo* commemoration issue shortly after his death, I wrote about the day, yes the day, when I read *Pedagogy of the Oppressed*, in 1973. It was indeed a cold Cuba, New Mexico day in early January. It had snowed all night. It would be a "snow day" for a young and very naïve second grade teacher. I wrote about the impact that one book—and, of course, the many that would follow–had on how I thought about and acted upon my life; about how my unseen contradictions became self-evident–contradictions that I held and still hold to this day, contradictions that I must have the courage to reveal by the actions that I take in the everyday. It is indeed an ever-evolving hermeneutic whereupon my actions on the world continue to expose the next contradictory dialectic unknown to me until I immerse myself in naming it, and with much practice, hopefully to transform it. I thought of my interactions with those around me; and, I thought about the learners that I was responsible for. I began to critique the many relationships, intended and otherwise, that impacted the construction of my person in a myriad of ways–a complexity of relationships that impact and are impacted by the realities we choose to create.

The dialectic of oppression and liberation became ever clearer to me as I read and reread quotes, pages, and sections that mattered most to me. These concepts will change and are dependent on what I am willing to critique and imagine for my own liberation with me and in tandem with the Other. However, and as difficult as it is to admit to this even today, in my early reading of *Pedagogy of the Oppressed*, I constructed oppression, and only oppression, as the dialectic. At that time I felt there were "oppressed" and "oppressors," never giving much thought to the notion that oppression (even though Paulo did explain this very concept), no matter how constructed and lived, was what it has always been: oppression–one side of the same coin. Even the last few pages of this momentous book did not cause me to rethink, in what is now an obvious lapse, what Paulo refers to as my magical thinking.

The dialectic, of course, was and continues to be a transformative dialectic. In my naïve thinking, one was either oppressed or an oppressor. Then, however, it was not clear what would occur once I rid myself of "that" oppression. As if by some miracle, I thought, I would awaken some day and be free, liberated, and full of some feeling of ecstasy. Freedom, in my mind, was not defined; I had no language for it other than it was something better than the racial, gender, and economic oppression I perceived and was unwittingly complicit with at that time. But for me, at that particular time and space, it was the getting rid of oppression that I, unknowingly and quite stupidly, was in fact further perpetuating–the invisible web of oppression.

T. Wilson, P. Park and A. Colón-Muñiz (eds.), Memories of Paulo, 101–104.
© 2010 Sense Publishers. All Rights Reserved.

This is my beginning with Paulo when he became part of me. These early remembrances formed the foundation of a scaffold of experiences, beginning with my initial memory of his impact upon me. Notwithstanding my obvious limitations about the profound dialectic Paulo set forth, the world became a new place; with all my limitations, I immersed myself into reading my world. Oppression was all around me, and for that matter, still is today. At that time, I unfortunately became bitter against what I had objectified as *the gringo* or *los gabachos* and *the system* that "they" were privy to–it was very much an "us" against "them" view that I had. I reasoned I was better than "they" were, somehow. As I continued to read Paulo's writings, I felt I was becoming "less oppressed," vague as that may be. Early in my journey, I failed to perceive the transformative complexity and humanistic altruism of Paulo's writings. The bitterness that I profoundly felt was actually bitterness towards my own blind complicity of accepting and, ever so subtly, falling into a perceived "lesser" status. I failed to decipher a cornerstone to Paulo's thinking that we are in this world together and that we are all human beings. It is truly embarrassing to admit that I accepted the idea of thinking of myself as less than what I indeed was and continue to be: a man, a Chicano by my political choice, a complex human being full of unfolding contradictions. By rereading and further absorbing Paulo's writings, I finally realized that this *thing* that sucked my living energy and self, which forced me to comply with a self-imposed deficit status, actually came from the inside. Yet, in the early years, I was not able to come to terms with this very simple and loving idea. I was not, at that time in my life, willing to accept responsibility for recognizing the stupidity of it all, neatly well-honed constructed hegemony so named the *ideology* of white supremacy; an ideology that *I* complied with. It was this ideology within me that I must disembowel; the transformative "act" of liberation, it seems to me, is to begin living this very personal commitment to the self, and by default, to the Other.

I go back now to *Pedagogy...* and the dialectic, which continues to reveal itself and sometimes, now more than ever, can be as clear as a summer monsoon day in New Mexico, with its white-grey clouds back-dropped with a blue southwestern sky. On a good day, the dialectic is unambiguous: the thesis is oppression and its many manifestations that I continue to name; the antithesis is liberation and *its* many manifestations that continue to be imagined and made "real" by my agency in the everyday; and when I am courageous enough to critique the contradiction, it is then fully revealed; *transformation* may then happen. The contradiction continues because we live almost all of our lives immersed in false consciousness that self-creates the ideology of white supremacy–what Karel Kosík (1976) in his masterful work *Dialectics of the concrete: A study on problems of Man and World,* names as the pseudo-concrete. Because we are part of humankind, immersed in what a "taker" ideology can do to warp our realities, revealing the contradiction by naming it is not what liberation is about. From my reading of Paulo and remembering his life albeit second hand, for I only met him once; hence, mostly through his writings, revealing a contradiction is only the first step. The step that follows, once named, is the transformative act, lest the oppressive contradiction will continue. Paulo said it so well back in the mid-1980s at a California State

University, Los Angeles forum on critical pedagogy; I paraphrase: *"Oppression is like an onion, it grows from the inside out and we peel the outer layer of oppression one layer at a time..."*

It is my action(s) upon the world that will begin to reveal the contradiction(s) to myself and to others and through my actions via that ever so small effort to live that "act" of transformation, the peeling of one layer of oppression one layer at a time, which, in the end, creates a "pedagogy of the oppressed." The dialectic within community and with my actions upon the world, small as they may seem, occur by my *showing* and not by my *telling*. The dialogue in community is nothing more than the explaining of the same phenomenon from a variety of spaces, each with its own time and reference.

At least at this point in time and with hindsight, Paulo has taught me to make meaning of this: that the journey we must embrace is indeed an evolutionary jaunt into ourselves becoming more human by the meaningful relationships and the cultural circles we courageously create based on the mutual understanding–said or unsaid–that we, each of us, is worthy and that no one is less than another. It is a working *axiom* in Paulo's works. A few months after my first reading of *Pedagogy,* I immersed myself in a *Harvard Educational Review* publication that would later become yet another small but monumental work: *Cultural Action for Freedom.* In Part II, "Cultural Action and Conscientization," footnote number six was one that I read over and over again and to this day continue to think about and to reread. It reads:

> In a discussion of men-world relationships during a 'circulo de cultura,' a Chilean peasant affirmed, 'I now see that there is no world without men.' When the educator asked, 'Suppose all men died, but there were still trees, animals, birds, rivers, and stars, wouldn't this be the world?' 'No,' replied the peasant, 'there would be no one to say, this is the world.' (1970, pp. 29–30)

> Rather than reproductive, our actions, our roles, as teachers and learners must be transformative. This is central to creating an opportunity for transformation by our living a 'pedagogy of the oppressed.' Naming the world around us then creates an opportunity for transformation to result. Through his writings, Paulo argues that we, both as teachers and as learners, must place ourselves within striking distance of the hotwires of the transformative dialectic. It is this tension that creates the democratic moment. 'It is a struggle between saying and doing,' Paulo writes in *Teachers as Cultural Workers: Letters to Those Who Dare Teach*, 'in which we must engage to diminish the distance between them, it is just as possible to change what is said to make it fit the doing as it is to change the doing to make it fit what is said.' (1998, p. 67)

In remembering Paulo, it is incumbent upon me to struggle to concretize my world in reflecting painfully at times on the ambiguity within myself where, as Paulo writes, "I feel I am not able to continue like this and I look for a way out [e]ither I change the progressivist discourse for a discourse consistent with my reactionary practice, or I change my practice for a democratic one, adapting it to the progressivist discourse." (p. 67) It is this moment in time–as teacher *and* as learner with the learners I am responsible to–that the democratic moment can happen if the latter is chosen. A non-choice is a choice; a choice is always present and thus the "pedagogy of the oppressed" continues...

REFERENCES

Freire, P. (2000). *Pedagogy of the oppressed.* London: Continuum International Publishers, Ltd.

Freire, P. (1998). *Teachers as cultural workers: Letters to those who dare teach* (D. Macedo, D. Koike, & A. Oliveira, Trans.). Boulder, CO: Westview Press.

Freire, P. (1970/1975). *Cultural action for freedom.* Cambridge, MA: Harvard Educational Review.

Kosík, K. (1976). *Dialectics of the concrete: A study on problems of Man and World.* In R. S. Cohen & M. W. Wartofsky (Eds.), and K. Kovanda with J. Schmidt (Trans.), *Boston studies in the philosophy of science* (Vol. LII). Boston: D. Reidel Publishing Company.

Rudolfo Chávez Chávez, Regents Professor
Department of Curriculum and Instruction
New Mexico State University, Las Cruces

MARK LYND

24. CONTROVERSY AND COMPLEXITY

When I got the notice from the University of Massachusetts that I had been accepted into their graduate program of education, I was elated–not only because this Southern California boy had an opportunity to study in New England with its legendary fall colors, but because my program, the Center for International Education, featured Paulo Freire as a guest faculty member. Freire had changed the way I viewed education. My own education had been characterized by sitting in rows in Catholic schools, working out of textbooks, and the "banking model" of education in high school and college, with teachers and professors filling me as an empty vessel. In my mid-20s, I became a Peace Corps volunteer in the Central African Republic where I taught high school English. During that time, I read *Pedagogy of the Oppressed* and something snapped: no longer was education simply a matter of transmitting information, but rather a key–perhaps *the* key–to changing the whole world. In particular, Freire's notion about dialogue as a means of developing critical thinking resonated with me. What a concept! Dialogue wasn't just something actors did in a play or people did over coffee, but something educators did to help their learners think critically about the world in order to change it! This became my primary mission. Instead of asking students to transform a text from the present to the past, I began to ask them to write essays on the reasons for conditions in their lives and in the world, and how they could be different (though, truth be told, to reward them, I would break out my guitar and lead them, yet again, in singing Roger Miller's "King of the Road").

So imagine my surprise when I saw Paulo for the first time. He was sitting in front of a group of graduate students, answering one question after another, for almost an hour. "OK," I said. "This is the man who reinvented the word 'dialogue.' Maybe he's just warming up." Another 15 minutes went by, and still the question-and-answer format. "When will the dialogue begin?" I was wondering when suddenly, a woman flung open the door, glanced around the packed room and found a chair tucked away in the corner. After about five more minutes of question and answer, she hopped up, strode to the chalk board and in broad capital letters wrote SEXISM, then returned to her seat. Freire looked at the blackboard, then went on to finish one of his famously long, philosophical answers, a murmur settling over the classroom. When he stopped, he turned to the woman and asked her what she meant. She replied in a crisp voice that throughout *Pedagogy of the Oppressed*, Paulo had exclusively used the word "he." (This was 1986, and *Pedagogy* had been published in 1973, but had since been reprinted.) His response: "Yes, I have been made aware of this many times and you're right, I am talking about men

T. Wilson, P. Park and A. Colón-Muñiz (eds.), Memories of Paulo, 105–108.
© *2010 Sense Publishers. All Rights Reserved.*

and women. But this is the way I wrote it. 'Man' in this case means people. I have been asked to change it but this is the way I wrote it. I want that we not talk about this any more."

My feeling of dismay about the lack of dialogue to that point changed to one of alarm: does he not get it? Does he not care? Has he just moved on to other issues in his quest for education for liberation? And why is he cutting off all conversation? This, the man who spoke of dialogue in *Pedagogy* with the eloquence of John's Gospel and "In the beginning was the word." I was baffled.

In time, I joined my friend and colleague, Peter Park, in the creation of a nonprofit organization called CCEA, or the Center for Community Education and Action. CCEA was dedicated to promoting participatory research in western Massachusetts. Peter had known Paulo for many years, and had been bringing him to the U.S. for workshops, conferences and university courses. One day, under the umbrella of CCEA, we organized a workshop for social activists in New England and brought Paulo in as a guest speaker. By now it was the late 80s and Paulo still had significant star appeal, particularly amongst leftists and radical educators. There were some 30 people–mostly women, as I remember–assembled in the meeting room of a church in Northampton, listening (again, listening) to Paulo talk about education for liberation, the revolution, etc., when his discourse took an unfortunate turn: "This is one problem I have with the revolution," he said. "Sometimes many women in the revolution, they do good things, but they carry guns, they wear uniforms, and they become fa-a-a-t and uuu-gly, with no maaaake-up. This I don't like. In Brazil, we like beautiful women. If you give me a choice between a revolutionary and a beautiful woman, I take the beautiful woman."

Imagine ALL of our surprise. Probably over half of the participants were women, of all sizes and shapes of course, many without makeup. After the now-routine silence following one of these gaffs, a friend (who wasn't wearing makeup) spoke up and said "I resent that. As a woman, I find that position unacceptable." Paulo responded, "No, no, you're not understanding me. I'm not talking about anyone here. I'm talking about women in the revolution who carry guns, who are fat and ugly and don't wear any makeup."

After the workshop, a few of us went to Peter's house to relax with Paulo and his wife, Nita and a few graduate students. We had some drinks and chatted about his stay in western Massachusetts. The feeling was jovial, we grad students feeling lucky to be in the presence of such an interesting and important personality. Paulo beamed when people asked questions, his eyes magnified by his glasses, thin, gray hair stroked back in professorial style. I sometimes had trouble understanding his English, spoken with a strong Portuguese accent, words often inverted. But in these soirees, or class meetings in people's homes with coffee brewing and flip charts papering the walls with words like "critical consciousness" and "hegemony," he was at his best, amongst his disciples, to be sure, painting pictures of work with peasants, literacy unlocking the imagination and the coming revolution, as if education were but one of many of the artist's brushes to be used in painting this grand picture. It energized all of us, Paulo's words combined with our commitment to "the struggle." It's an energy that I carry with me to this day.

But if I've been inspired by Paulo's warmth and ideas, knowing him has also been a lesson for me about the complexity of humanity. I was with him in those classes and soirees when he was loving, sharing, encouraging, even enlightening. I was also with him when he was bafflingly obtuse. After the workshop in Northampton, Paulo, Nita, Peter and I went out to dinner. It was a lovely time, each of us sharing stories of where we had been, experiences as educators working in Africa, Asia and Latin America. Yet the incident in the church in Northampton was gnawing at me. At one point, I seized a pause in the conversation and gingerly broached the subject again: "I'm not sure I understand what you meant about women in the revolution and..." Before I could finish, Paulo responded, "No, no, no, you didn't understand me. I said it in the meeting, I wasn't talking about anybody here, I was talking about women in the revolution. OK, I want that we not talk about this anymore."

My impression of Paulo as inspired, yet at times obtuse, was confirmed most poignantly in a conference for social activists held in Minnesota in the early 90s. The conference had been organized by a woman who had created a successful center for battered women using Paulo's ideas of dialogues, codes and generative themes in order to change their life situations. The conference featured Paulo as its guest speaker. In one session I attended, a group of counselors who work with batterers were asking Paulo numerous questions about how to raise consciousness about battering in order to change behavior. Question after question was met with "What do you mean?" or "In Brazil, we don't beat our women, we make love to them," (this after a recent 60 Minutes exposé on the murder of women being dismissed in Brazilian courts in the name of men's honor). At one point, exasperated, the counselors realized he wasn't getting it, so they staged a role play in which a counselor asked a batterer why he had beaten his wife. "I didn't," he said. "I just pushed her." "But the police report says her arm was broken," the counselor replied. "That's because she fell down the stairs," said the batterer. After a bit of this, the counselors stopped the role play, then turned to Paulo and asked what he would do. Paulo was aghast. "This happens in this country, like this?" he said. Everyone nodded vigorously. "I would kill the man," he said. By the end of the conference, word had gotten around that Paulo was not proving to be the luminary that the activists had been led to expect. It got so bad that in one of the final plenary sessions, conference participants were hurling questions at the organizer of the conference, asking why she had brought Paulo in the first place. She stood up and said "Listen, this is the man who wrote *Pedagogy of the Oppressed*, whose ideas we used to create our center. He's changed my life and he's changed theirs. This man has powerful ideas–he's my man–and I think he deserves to be listened to."

But the participants were never satisfied and I remember leaving that conference feeling that perhaps Paulo's light was flickering–that many of us, though forever changed by his ideas, could not understand this behavior. I believed he was doing his best, and to this day continue to believe in his ideas about how education can create a better world. Yet as I got to know him, I realized that he was perhaps confused about the rules of a world that seemed increasingly unfamiliar to him–a world inhabited by students like me who were searching not for strategies to work with Brazilian peasants, but to work with pernicious forms of institutionalized oppression that affect us all. It was this realization that finally led me to the conclusion, sadly, that in matters concerning the world *I* was trying to change, I would never be able to fully engage "the master."

REFERENCES

Freire, P. (2000). *Pedagogy of the oppressed.* London: Continuum International Press.
Freire, P. (1973). *Pedagogy of the oppressed.* New York: The Seabury Press, Inc.

Mark Lynd

JOHN RIVERA

25. PAULO'S DREAM

"Creating a New Moment in History"

My upbringing included a deep appreciation for the value of my indigenous and Chicano cultural heritage. As a young collegiate, I was introduced to Paulo Freire and ever since have marveled at his ability to work among so many different people and organizations to promote justice, from the cultural elites at Harvard, to the poor and formally uneducated in Brazil, and with governments on the left and the right.

Here in the U.S., we have a very special kind of democracy that was and is framed to protect both the majority and minority from tyranny. As we well know, however, we have a long way to go to correct past injustices and reach the promise of that ideal. Paulo explored and employed his experiences and many aspects of human expression to promote his dream of social justice.

Paulo's life has inspired me as I have sought to build upon and use my back-ground to inform the course of justice. As a child, I worked the farms picking summer fruit with my family. Later, I had the opportunity to be part of Cesar Chavez' farm worker movement. Paulo's work ultimately encouraged me to work on policy with the City Council in San Diego, California and to work in education with primary and secondary schools where the unjust neglect has existed for far too many generations; also with elite students at private universities, and community college students on probation.

In the 80s and 90s I had the privilege of meeting Paulo on several occasions in my work with the Institute for Education in Transformation, which began in the early 80s hosting activities and guests that exemplified the best of critical theorists. I would like to offer my personal reflections on Paulo, by revisiting some inter-views with him filmed in July of 1992.[1] I was especially drawn to Paulo's certainty that the solutions to issues of racism and other inequities will come only when we "create" a new moment in history where unity can emerge.

It always seemed to me that Paulo's praxis made him a practical, sensible man, while his love helped make him a dreamer–a powerful combination! By the time I met him, he had come to a different balance between "hating injustice" and loving justice in ways that could, and would, result in things being different at some point in history, in which he "created a new history."

I also experienced Paulo as a very loving man. I was drawn by how he could hate injustice with such strength and yet leave me with a vision for doing the work with the high standard of what he called a strong love. He could lean on your shoulder after dinner when he was tired and express his deep appreciation for a

T. Wilson, P. Park and A. Colón-Muñiz (eds.), Memories of Paulo, 109–113.
© 2010 Sense Publishers. All Rights Reserved.

flower arrangement, or an unusual cloud formation; he could gaze at Nita with deep tenderness, or exalt the beauty of a rubber plant worker's dialogue. His love was not "sweet love like water," he said but a strong love that fortified his courage and honesty and opened many doors for him all over the world in every imaginable milieu. He also developed the skills to maximize those opportunities to promote his dream of social justice.

During the last half century, attempts to develop critical theory in the U.S. through higher education, critical multiculturalism and ethnic, cultural, race, gender and critical studies programs would have realized more of the people's hopes and taken the world much further, had the struggle also included more of Paulo's strong love. I found Pauloian love is helpful and at times even essential when living through the hatred and depression that can sometimes accompany working critically with injustice.

Decades ago, David Mura warned about unproductive anger; he said at first it was liberating, then intoxicating and finally, damaging.[2] In contrast, there is a righteous anger that flows from genuine love. This has helped me sustain a vision for critically addressing injustice while encouraging others to develop a healthy balance between hatred for injustice and love for justice.

Four concepts of Paulo's response in the recorded videos strike me as bearing potential for guiding us in our efforts to build on this work "in our moment in history." I would like to talk with Paulo about these today, over a plate of *carnitas* and arugula salad (his favorites when he was with us). A good sign of new possibilities is that now (though not then) both dishes can be ordered at one restaurant!

INTENTIONAL ALLIANCES WITH SHARED GOALS

"The Color of Ideology"

I am not as sanguine as Paulo about the possibility of progress if we choose our liaison partners based on the color of their ideology any more than if we choose them based on the color of their skin. There are other signs that potential alliances can be created where people of all colors can come together around Paulo's dream and formulate shared goals for addressing racism and other inequities.

Paulo has pointed out that there is no such thing as working outside the system; he called it "an illusion," but still we must do what can be done in the moments we have. I believe that if we were to consciously improve our ability to develop intentional alliances, without giving up that which is core, more like Paulo did, enhanced progress could be made. When I look at Paulo, I see a man who is admired across the world today precisely because he could inspire very different people who lived very different lives. He challenged European and American intellectual elites in the universities from Boston, such as Harvard, to Paris and also challenged peasants and newly placed people of color like me working in our cities and communities. I always try to remember, as I go about my work, in what might look like a fragmented life that Paulo worked with peasants, students, universities, and institutions like the World Council of Churches. He was both exiled, and hired, by the Brazilian government. Like Nelson Mandela, Paulo knew how to talk to those who had been his enemies as well as to his friends.

Critical intellectuals and advocates can work to better model the spirit in which Paulo used the dialectic to have meaningful conversations that allowed him to help others care more about justice. Critical educators have done extremely important analyses, often contributing illuminating critique with little effect on actual practice.

Paulo dove right into the praxis of teaching peasants and working on public policy as Minister of Education. How I wish I could hear him now narrate that experience. Though he rarely discussed that experience when he was here, it was clear that Paulo knew that actionable theory and policy could only be developed from the ground up. For example, I remember hearing him tell how he had the children write and draw about school; parents would come and talk with him when he first began his education post.

To formulate new possibilities in our alliances, we can continue sharing what is, and what could be, including a stronger love; and then form a multi-faceted set of strategies that could be carried out by different parts of the alliance to achieve different, but mutually-supportive, goals among different constituencies. In this way, we could be more confident that we have found available common ground on which to unite those who sincerely care about justice.

Paulo's life and work provide a standard for us to reach toward as he explored, lived and taught the rich possibilities latent in the dialectic of paradoxes; such as his reflections on rigor and joy, authority and democracy, the poor and the rich, and the left and the right.

SACRIFICE AND HISTORY

"Not Anger or Guilt"

Paulo accurately observed that productive alliances must consist of people who have overcome anger and guilt to similar degrees. Paulo's love helped him to balance these emotions. He was arrested, humiliated, and exiled for seventeen years for his work with the poor. His life helps us to appreciate those who suffer and sacrifice rightly. He could have easily turned his suffering into rage against others or turned it on himself as guilt but he chose the higher path. He conquered adversity in a spirit of forgiveness, understanding, humility, grace and love. The joy that resulted energized him and was contagious to others. These are the tools I need also. As a result of all that happened to him and his quick mind and open heart, Paulo developed an uncanny sense of history that supported his ability to understand anger and guilt early in life. I was taught a similar history lesson by my great grandfather who urged me to think first of how every word and deed may affect people seven generations in the future.

Paulo reminds us that progress in history will require people to sacrifice their anger and guilt "because history does that." White people concerned with racism may have to sacrifice in different areas and in different ways than people of color.

Like Paulo, people of color must also sacrifice by loving those we view as averse. Jay Swallow, Chief of the Cheyenne Nation, says that we must no longer pass on our pain to our grandchildren. It can be a sacrifice to give up uncritical anger for it has often become a comforting and excusing companion. In order to sacrifice humbly, Whites may need to search for understanding of the injustice others experience, and work in isolation from a majority of their peers. This reminder of Paulo's helps me appreciate the Whites who worked alongside Martin Luther King, whose names we don't even know. They sacrificed some of their comfort and privilege to join the work of justice. Like them, white people today who care about justice can sacrifice guilt and the half-heartedness that causes them to hide insincerely behind the words of the latest "politically correct" doctrine. Paulo taught us that, with diligence and a proper hate and love, the rich and poor, the left and right, and Whites and people of color can live the sacrifice that the work of justice requires.

HONESTY

"Love is not Sweet like Water"

In these alliances we must become transparently honest with one another. We must learn to love those who have substantively different views on how to achieve justice. It has been said: What good is it if you love those who love you? Does not everyone love those that love them? That is the "love like water" that Paulo describes. When we can come to a place where we have strong love, we will have a stronger foundation for justice and a healthy freedom. We will be able to go far beyond the ideologies of the day, beyond the pat expressions of political correctness and the easy arrogance sometimes found in conservatism and progressivism. Paulo did this with humility and honesty; both of these challenge me to continue the difficult journey to become authentic with others and myself as I try to remain in the classroom of humility. Mother Teresa said that it takes a lot of humiliation to get just a little humility. To work within a true diversity of ideologies and world-views there will be a great need for both. Recognizing the good and holding ourselves accountable for our mistakes, we can begin to develop and initiate new possibilities for justice in all aspects of individual and social life. Then, as Paulo exhorted us, "the time will have come for unity."

MEASURE RESULTS AGGRESSIVELY

"Explained Scientifically"

Paulo considered himself a scientist and believed that science could be helpful in revealing where and when we were right or wrong, if we can find ways to measure our results scientifically. He said "racism is unscientific." Critical and other "leftist" educators now lead some of the major national research organizations in education. This gives an opportunity to make scientific research work for promoting justice in education.

Paulo helped instill a desire in me, and in others, to do the kind of research needed to see if our theories are working in the real world, in praxis; but we have yet to develop our fullest potential in this area. Education, in particular, is a field full of journal articles making great proclamations supported by little data. We can make abstract excuses for this, provide structural reasons, and offer powerful ideological explanations, but, in the end, we still need to know the effect of our work.

We can apply more relevantly some of the measures currently used by conservative colleagues; we can help more skillfully correct measurement flaws and develop new measures that more accurately evaluate progress toward justice and excellence. Paulo, the scientist, acted strongly; I hope that we can develop more ways to strongly measure our hopes and honestly face our progress and our failures, so that we build justice on solid ground rather than shifting sands.

When I think of Paulo now, I am grateful for his hatred of injustice and love of justice, his humility and boldness, his rigor and joy. He seemed so comfortable with paradox, and perhaps it was because he had highly unified these and other paradoxes within his own soul.

Paulo was not afraid to question, not afraid to be wrong, not afraid to let someone of a different ideology, color, or economic status help transform his mind, not afraid to work with whomever, whenever and wherever possible, and most importantly he was not afraid to tell the truth about what he believed even if it meant we wouldn't "love him."

These are qualities that will help sustain a life of struggle for justice and work with diverse people and groups. These qualities will help us to live the sacrifice and will help us to develop intentional alliances required to create a new, better, moment in history.

NOTES

[1] The quotations from Paulo herein are from two hour-long videos filmed in 1992 which are currently being produced and will be made available through the Institute. For further information write to Professor Mary Poplin, The Institute for Education in Transformation, School of Educational Studies, Claremont Graduate University, Claremont, CA 91711

[2] David Mura, Strangers in the Village. In Rick Simonson & Scott Walker, *The Graywolf Annual Five: Multicultural Literacy* (Saint Paul, MN: Graywolf Press, 1988).

John Rivera, Ph.D., Director
Policy at the Institute for Education in Transformation
Claremont Graduate University

ROBERT W. HOWARD

26. MEMORIES OF PAULO

Cambridge, Irvine, and New Orleans

As I enter my office at the University of Washington, Tacoma and walk towards my desk, I encounter a framed poster that reminds me of a powerful experience that I, and several others, shared with Paulo Freire. I did not have the good fortune to spend as much time with Paulo as did many of the contributors to this volume. The first time I met Paulo was in March 1985, when I saw Paulo speak in Longfellow 100 at the Harvard Graduate School of Education. That evening, Paulo demonstrated an emotional commitment to his philosophy and beliefs and held a standing-room only audience riveted during his presentation and subsequent dialogue with several members of the group.

The last time I saw Paulo before his death was at the 1995 Association for Supervision and Curriculum Development (ASCD) conference in New Orleans. Either by chance or someone at ASCD having an ironic sense of humor in scheduling, Paulo's presentation in a large auditorium was followed in the next block of sessions by William J. Bennett, former United States Secretary of Education and well-known political conservative. Because so many people felt the need to approach Paulo at the end of his session, Bennett was standing alone at the podium as Paulo left the auditorium accompanied by many conference participants. I cannot quote Bennett verbatim, but as I recall the event, he looked disdainfully at Paulo and made a comment about waiting for a rock star and his groupies to leave the hall. (What baffled *me* was wondering why, given the *possibility* of dialogue with Paulo, any conference participant would choose to stay in the hall with the *certainty* of a didactic address from Bill Bennett.)

The most extended exposure I had to Paulo was during a week-long Dialogue with Paulo event held at the University of California, Irvine (UCI) in July 1987. It seems to me–with a potentially mistaken memory of the details–that we had a group of about 75 people. While my memory about the number of participants may be faulty, several events and aspects of the week were powerful and unforgettable. We were a very diverse group, but shared an interest in social justice and an appreciation for the philosophy and pedagogy of Paulo Freire.

Of the events of the week, none for me was more powerful than the strong sense of community that quickly developed through Freirean dialogue. We were able to not only raise questions about the unconscious *isms* that we saw play out in the words and actions of others, but also could see them in ourselves without becoming paralyzed by our own psychological defenses. During the week, we had opportunities

T. Wilson, P. Park and A. Colón-Muñiz (eds.), Memories of Paulo, 115–117.
© *2010 Sense Publishers. All Rights Reserved.*

to talk with Paulo informally. I remember lamenting, during a lunch with Paulo and a small group at a Mexican restaurant near the campus, about the quality of Mexican food in Cambridge and Boston (where I was then living). I was surprised that in each of our experiences in the Bay State, both Paulo and I considered the possibility of opening restaurants in the area to address what we saw as a critical need and a gastronomic vacuum.

The poster hanging in my office is a result of the week at UCI. It is a poster produced from a silk screen which Paulo had seen at the previous year's Dialogue with Paulo. Tom Wilson and his colleagues, in organizing the 1987 Dialogue, secured permission to use the silk screen in publicizing and commemorating the week-long event, and produced posters. Added at the bottom of the poster version of the silk screen are the name of the event, date, and a memorial to Paulo's wife Elza, who had died in the year between the UCI Dialogues. In terms of the content of the painting, in the center of the work is a brown-skinned human in profile and with a large and colorful eye. This character is portrayed such that from one perspective it is in a fetal position; from another perspective, in supplication; from a third in meditation and reflection. The figure's expression is hard to interpret, but three flowers–one as part of a necklace, one near the character's mouth, and one in the foreground–strike me as positive and hopeful.

As my eye scans the art, I am drawn first to the human character, second to the flowers, then finally to the upper third of the painting where I realize that the white form, initially dwarfed by the vivid colors, is a soaring bird. I see the bird as representing the potential for liberation from any current oppressive reality. While the work of art is powerful, it probably would not hang in such a noticeable place in my office if it had not been for Paulo's reaction to the piece and our reaction to him.

On the final morning of the conference, we participants were anxiously awaiting a long session with Paulo at the front of the room. Before Paulo began what would have been a presentation and large-group dialogue, Tom Wilson introduced the artist who was responsible for the silk screen that became the symbol for the week's Dialogue. The artist unveiled the original work and made a gift of it to Paulo. Paulo was so emotionally moved by the gift that he broke down in tears. Tom suggested that we give Paulo some time and that we reconvene as a large group in fifteen minutes.

At that point, Tom was alone at the front of the room and explained that Paulo was so affected by the gift and the associated memories, that he had returned to his hotel room and that he would not be joining the group for the long session that had been scheduled. Tom continued and told us that he (Tom) had to be in a meeting elsewhere at UCI virtually immediately and that we would need to decide how best to use the time. We were faced, in Paulo's terms, with an experience of *problem posing* education. That we formed such bonds in the community served us well. Several groups formed based on interest areas. My choice was, with a colleague from the Boston area, to examine issues of indoctrination and colonialism.

On a superficial level, from the experience of the day, I learned that if you plan to do something with the potential of raising powerful emotions in your featured speaker, do it at the end of the session rather than at the outset. Pedagogically,

I realized that within a week, we had formed community and critical consciousness. In that context, we were liberated and able to make autonomous decisions and act on them.

Occasionally, I wonder if the same would be true, under similar circumstances, of the group in New Orleans who stayed in the room to hear Bill Bennett rather than join Paulo in dialogue. Would they be as understanding and be so liberated and autonomously directed? An empirical question to be sure, but I would be willing to make a small wager that the situation would be different.

Robert W. Howard, Associate Professor
Education Program
University of Washington, Tacoma

TOM STICHT

27. THE LEGACY OF PAULO FREIRE

(1921–1997)

My personal knowledge of Paulo Freire comes from the nine years—1987 through 1996–during which I worked one week each year with him when we both served as members of UNESCO's International Jury for Literacy Prizes. Already an international giant of adult literacy education when he joined the Jury in 1987, Paulo brought his philosophy of literacy for liberation and freedom to the evaluation of candidates for literacy prizes from countries where millions of adults were oppressed. He brought a passion to the evaluation of candidates often expressed by clenching his hands in a fist, clutching his chest and saying, "I love this program!" He was also quick to provide a critical commentary when he thought that a program had mistakenly claimed that it followed "the Freirean method," and he admonished the Jury that there was no such method. During the Jury's deliberations regarding candidatures, and on our breaks when we would take tea or coffee, I had occasions to listen to him and to talk informally with him about his philosophy of education and literacy, and how he had worked early on in his career with the poor and oppressed peasants of Brazil. Of course, in his own early literacy work he did use certain techniques such as discussing pictures to elicit knowledge from learners to help them to read the world, and to obtain so-called "generative words" used to further stimulate thought. But apparently he did not think of this as a particular "method," though others have focused upon these techniques and referred to them as the "Freirean method." In actuality, Freire took a functional stance toward literacy. Like most of the other members of the Jury, he regarded literacy as a means to an end, not an end in itself. In his work he considered literacy as a means of helping adults liberate themselves from oppression imposed by others, such as government forces, landlords, corrupt business operators and the like.

To do this he first concentrated on teaching adults to "read the world" so they could then "read the word." By "reading the world" he meant helping adults understand the differences between the world of nature and the world of culture. Nature is made by natural forces, and is not subject to change by humans. Culture, on the other hand, is made by humans and can be changed by humans. We "read the world" to know what is nature and what is culture. Oppressive conditions are cultural, and hence capable of being changed by humans. Literacy for Freire was viewed as a technology for helping humans change the cultural contexts in which they live, so that they can achieve social justice, and is hence worthwhile learning. Freire contrasted this learner-centered, participatory approach in which the adults helped

T. Wilson, P. Park and A. Colón-Muñiz (eds.), Memories of Paulo, 119–120.

determine the content and direction of their own education within the contexts of their immediate perceived needs and contextual situations, with the more traditional, school-centered education which is so prevalent in adult literacy education in industrialized nations today. In most of these nations, there have been movements toward the development of "content standards" and a scope and sequence of knowledge and skills in which adult learners progress from lower to higher levels of literacy. This was considered by Freire as antithetical to his ideas of the contextual functionality of literacy. He denounced as inappropriate to the stimulation of human liberation such approaches to curriculum development in which policymakers, administrators or teachers determine the content and direction of education and attempt to deposit and "bank" knowledge in learners' minds even if they do not understand the value of the new knowledge. Today, millions of adults and their families around the world live in constant fear that they will not have adequate water, food, health care and security for their very lives. Many live in conditions of economic and political oppression, and they may perceive that they have little chance of changing their lives in any significant manner. For this reason they may elect to stay away from literacy classes. They see no use for literacy in their lives. In these circumstances, Freire's approach to adult literacy education, if not a method, as he would claim, is nonetheless an approach that can instill a feeling of confidence in adult learners and motivate them to engage in literacy learning. In 1975 Paulo Freire was awarded a UNESCO Literacy Prize for his work on the *Pedagogy of the Oppressed*. Over a quarter century later, in 2003, a non-governmental organization called the International Reflect Circle (CIRAC) was awarded a UNESCO literacy prize for its work which built upon the work of Freire. The acronym REFLECT stands for Regenerated Freirean Literacy through Empowering Community Techniques. The REFLECT approach to adult literacy development makes use of "multiple literacies," much as did Freire in using pictures and other graphic tools to help adults "read the world." To assist adults in capturing their own knowledge, the REFLECT teachers show them how to make maps of their communities, construct matrices, flow charts, and other graphics to analyze their needs and assist them in arguing for needed services and social justice. REFLECT makes use of internet technologies and has formed an international network of some 350 organizations and individuals in 60 nations to facilitate sustainable community development using a participatory and democratic process of reflection by adults in the development of their own literacy education. Through the work of REFLECT and numerous other groups around the world, Paulo Freire's learner-centered, participatory approach to adult literacy education continues to help marginalized, socially excluded adults develop the confidence and abilities they need to not just "read the world," but to change it. This is an enduring legacy of the work of Paulo Freire.

Thomas G. Sticht
International Consultant in Adult Education
El Cajon, California

HELEN M. LEWIS

28. PAULO FREIRE AT HIGHLANDER

In December 1987, Paulo Freire came to the Highlander Center, an adult education center in East Tennessee, to "talk a book" with Myles Horton, the founder of Highlander. They met at a conference in California earlier that year and Paulo asked Myles to consider "speaking a book," a method Paulo had used to develop some of his books. They were both considered pioneers in the development of non-formal, popular education, education for social change and a pedagogy which evolved into Participatory Action Research. Although they had briefly met at several conferences, they had never had the opportunity to spend time together, to compare their experiences and their ideas.

Their friends and colleagues saw the possibilities this would provide to get these two educator-activists together to share their ideas and to make these available to educators throughout the world. Sue Thrasher of the Highlander staff mobilized the staff and friends at the University of Tennessee who arranged for Paulo to come to the Highlander Center and meet with Myles at his home at the Highlander Center on the side of Bays Mountain.

They settled in around the fireplace, with the Great Smoky Mountains as a backdrop. Some friends and members of Highlander staff listened and acted more as clarifiers and prompters than as interviewers. Both men were great story tellers so those of us who sat with them mostly listened as they got to know each other, shared their experiences, questioned each other, compared their own development, change of ideas and educational philosophy.

We also observed two people, who had known about each other but had never really spent time getting to know each other, develop a deep and lasting friendship. The conversations were both relaxed and spontaneous and developed into what has been described as "a dance between old companions accustomed to the subtle leads and responses by one, then the other." (*We Make the Road by Walking* p. ix) It was like watching two people discovering each other with feeling and respect. They were excited and amazed at the many commonalities, how they both came to similar analyses, despite differences in cultural contexts. It was like watching two old men falling in love.

During this visit, I was on staff at Highlander and working with rural communities trying to rebuild their communities which had lost their industrial base of mining. We invited some of these community leaders to come meet Paulo and talk with each other about their community development work. Paulo was excited to

T. Wilson, P. Park and A. Colón-Muñiz (eds.), Memories of Paulo, 121–123.

meet these grassroots leaders, mostly women, who–with the help of Highlander educational programs–had analyzed their experiences, developed their own under-standing of the causes of their problems and had created some unique community programs.

One of the exercises at the workshop with Paulo and Myles was drawing a picture of the relationship between their community and the Highlander Center. Maxine Waller from Ivanhoe, Virginia drew a picture which included a goat on the hill looking down on the workshop at the Center which she explained was Myles Horton observing the educational process and occasionally butting in to push for more analysis.

Paulo was delighted with this description of Myles' educational methodology for empowerment. He was excited to validate what he had long believed, that the methods he used with peasants in Third World countries also worked in the First World, too.

The process of "talking a book" became intensely personal and therapeutic for both men. It renewed their strength and gave them a new sense of possibility and hope. Myles was 82 years old, 16 years older than Paulo. He was not an academic or a writer as Paulo was, and had not really published much about his pedagogy. This provided an outlet to express his ideas and he saw it as a way to get his and Paulo's ideas about education available to more people. Paulo credited his reflections with Myles as helping to bring him out of his despair over Elza's death. He said, "At Highlander I began to read and to write again." (p. xxxi) Back home in Brazil he became involved in the political struggles and became Secretary of Education in São Paulo working to transform a traditional education system there.

When they finished their conversations they agreed that they had said all they needed to say. Paulo concluded, "I think it will be a beautiful book." Myles said, "Let's have a drink." (p. 248)

Brenda Bell, John Gaventa, and John Peters edited the conversations into a manuscript and titled it *We Make the Road by Walking: Conversations on Education and Social Change*. The title came from an observation made by Paulo at the beginning of the conversations. He adapted a quote from the Spanish poet Antonio Machado saying "I am sure that we make the road by walking."

Two years after the conversations in January 1990, Paulo returned to Highlander to visit Myles. The plan was for them to review the manuscript draft and possibly add or make revisions. Myles' cancer had recurred and he was very ill. Myles had struggled to be alert and have enough energy to work with Paulo. They had several short conversations and agreed that the manuscript was almost ready. They together expressed pleasure with the form it had taken. But the situation was very emotional.

When Paulo saw his friend, he said the work on the book was not the agenda for this meeting. It was to be with his friend in his last days. Myles relaxed and enjoyed Paulo's friendship and support. They ate together and looked out over the mountains and the birds in the feeder. Paulo commented: "It is sad, but dying is a necessary part of living. It is wonderful that Myles may die here, ...dying in the midst of life." (p xxxiii) It was their last conversation. Three days after Paulo left, Myles slipped into a coma and died Jan 19, 1990. The book was published by Temple University Press later in the year.

REFERENCES

Horton, M., Friere, P., Bell, B., Gaventa, J., & Peters, J. (Eds.). (1990). *We make the road by walking: Conversations on education and social change.* Philadelphia: Temple University Press.

Helen M. Lewis
Retired Highlander Staff
Morganton, Georgia

ESTHER PÉREZ

29. FREIRE, CUBAN STYLE

I met Paulo Freire in 1987, in what some would consider a typical situation in Havana. He had come to Cuba for the first time, invited as a special guest to give a master lecture, but due to an oversight or a mix-up nobody went to pick him up at the airport. A sympathetic taxi driver dropped him off at a hotel.

From there Paulo did what many other intellectuals of his generation must have done before him when stuck in a similar situation: he looked in the telephone book for Casa de las Américas, headquarters for the guild of lost writers, stray poets and misplaced essayists. Roberto ended up taking the call, yelling loud enough to be heard in Sao Paulo, until he realized that Paulo was only in the Tritón Hotel and just wanted some help to get to the conference.

When all was straightened out and communication reestablished between guest and hosts, Roberto thought that I should conduct an interview with Paulo to be published in the journal *Casa de las Américas*. The reason for doing the interview was clear: the journal was gaining in prestige and this was an "exclusive." After all, we had been the first to find out about the semi-clandestine arrival of Paulo Freire in Cuba. The reason I was chosen requires further explanation: Casa de las Américas at that time was trying to revitalize its interest in popular education, which had arisen in the early 1980s, and they had assigned me this almost sacred mission, the inspiration for which was provided by Frei Betto, who would end up changing my life, as I would go on to dedicate myself full time to popular education.

Paulo Freire, Fernando Martínez and I ended up having scrambled eggs and ham at the table in my house, and we recorded the interview with a borrowed tape recorder.

In the end it turned out well, as he preferred, and as he surely would have planned–if these things turn out better when planned and not left to unfold naturally–an episode in which form and content corresponded exactly, or better yet, in which the form was a perfect metaphor of the content. Because the reality is that Paulo Freire was unknown in Cuba, except for small groups that had the good fortune to discover his books published abroad, or run into him, or his work, or his followers, or his name in this or that occasional meeting.

I met Paulo again on two other occasions. The first–a fleeting on–in Brazil, during his seventieth birthday. It was a very large reunion in which we, the guests, passed one by one in front of the table where he was seated–like a sick martyr who submits to the tributes. The second was also in São Paulo, in December of that following year, and once again, like the first time, the occasion was set up, but this time more directly, by Frei Betto. He invited the six of us (Cuban women who had

T. Wilson, P. Park and A. Colón-Muñiz (eds.), Memories of Paulo, 125–132.
© 2010 Sense Publishers. All Rights Reserved.

come to participate in an exchange with Brazilian Popular Education centers) to lunch, and in the middle of the conversation he asked us if we would like to meet with Paulo. So we went, the next day, to his house, where this time we were able to have a long conversation with the obviously fragile–but still lucid–old man, about his latest book, about his experience as São Paulo's Secretary of Education during the government of the Workers Party, about the development of his ideas after *Pedagogy of Hope* and about his next trip to Cuba –the second, which he never took– [scheduled for] May of 1997.

He was the one who mentioned the Havana interview and he asked if I would send him a copy, because he had lost his own copy during a move. He told me he needed it because he felt that in it he had expressed for the first time intuitions that were developed in his later work of the 1990s. I never sent it to him because I didn't have the opportunity, and, since I was expecting to see him in Havana a few months later, I decided that handing it to him personally would be a good excuse for us to engage in another conversation. He died two days before the scheduled date of his second visit to Cuba. With his death, the Brazilian intellectual community and the Brazilian people lost, in one year's time, the second of two great leaders, two wise thinkers of our time, two founders of Latin American science and consciousness for the world. Paulo Freire was connected in this way as well to Darcy Ribeiro.

Since then I have reread that 1988 interview a number of times looking for what Paulo would have wanted to rediscover in it, and I think I know what it is. Starting with the explanation of the idea of the *politicality* or political nature of education, present in his reflections since the very beginning with *Education as a Practice of Freedom*, he examines his association with different contemporary revolutionary processes (Guinea-Bissau, Granada, Nicaragua...) and his political affiliation in the Workers Party. To him this involvement didn't arise separately, alongside his practice as an educator, but rather as an integral part of the practice as a whole. That's why his reflections on dialogical pedagogy mix, as they do in life, with his views on politics. In the interview we see the complete, mature Paulo Freire, who thinks of his practice as a revolutionary educator–as he liked to define himself–in terms of the whole.

But beyond the personal memories–those of us who knew him or read his work have already come together to share stories–it's important to say something about Paulo for those who never knew him, those who still don't know him, those who are going to discover him some day in *Pedagogy of the Oppressed* or *Letters from Guinea-Bissau*.

How does one answer the question of who Paulo Freire really was, why he deserves tributes, commemorations, reunions? He was, first and foremost, a revolutionary Latin American intellectual, a social thinker and not a school reformer, although some would like to reduce him to the latter. He was an intellectual from his first writings, from "way back" in the sixties; his critics called the writings idealist, an adjective that he perhaps too generously accepted and turned into a cause for introspection and self-critique. He was an intellectual because he placed as much importance on the socialization of his discoveries as on the discoveries themselves. He was an inspiration, for many, for different reasons. I'll mention a few of the ones that motivate me.

To begin with, Paulo Freire reclaimed the intellectual condition and its specific functions, the importance of thinking about and for revolutionary processes. And he acted on this determination amid criticism and lack of understanding, maintaining a consistency throughout his life. To bring about a new society there had to be–as he stated and exemplified through his life's work–a thinking process dedicated to this goal, which *is an integral part* of the praxis. To start from a real life practice and reflect on it in order to achieve a transformed practice was one of his central ideas. And education could be an excellent vehicle to allow more and more people to join this practice of action and thought that he put forth and lived.

Secondly, he laid the foundations for a way of thinking about education that spread from Latin America to the rest of the world, although it was specifically continental in that it originated in the analysis of the school system and the learning processes as they existed in Latin America at that time. His dialogic pedagogy is one of the great contributions of Latin American intellectuals to humanity, and Paulo also had the privilege of personally contributing in other areas as well, notably in Africa.

Third, he focused his reflections on a crucial area: on the necessary reconstruction of the political so that it might transcend the limits of *governability* and become the place where the public and the private, the rational and the affective, the complete human being come together, the place of enormous complexity that liberation or liberatory thinking has to be viable and attractive. This initial understanding–in his very first books he was talking about liberation pedagogy–which came early in his case and was, therefore, a source of criticism at the time, has proven with the passage of time to be one of the keys to the necessary rethinking of the political, a difficult problem which the revolutions and other left political practices of the 21st century will have to deal with in all its complexity. In his Havana interview he addressed this topic.

He also laid the foundation for a popular pedagogy that, because it was genuinely and profoundly popular, was always anti-dogmatic and anti-sectarian, open to the input of all, aware of negative participation, but intrinsically open to the contribution of the different, and based on such a contribution, it even favored permanent curiosity, risk and change. But he didn't set his discoveries in stone. He said that the contributions of earlier pedagogy had to be consumed, metabolized, incorporated into our own pedagogical practice, because it was on these shoulders, not in a vacuum, that we stood.

He knew that only social and political engagement could create a complete person, that values were not passed on but rather created and recreated by each succeeding generation, which must form new values through its own engagement and struggle, equal and different, going beyond the praxes of earlier generations.

Speaking of his life upon the occasion of his death, many have praised his consistency. And it's true: he was consistent with the truths he was discovering; with the social and political processes in which he participated, although sometimes he might do so through fraternal disagreement; with the popular education movement, who proclaimed him their intellectual inspiration, and with whom they always maintained an intense and affectionate debate. I would like to point out, however, another manifestation of his consistency that seems to me of great importance. I'm referring to the consistency he maintained between his intellectual positions and his life's work.

Convinced of his option for the popular, he engaged in a process of thorough questioning with the people of Latin America without ever giving in to the temptation of taking the easy or simple way out. His search was always multiple, astute and profound.

Conscious of our need to develop fully as human beings so that we are capable of establishing the political on new foundations, he built his character and conducted himself with great care. Well educated, he could have a conversation with anybody without ever being condescending; famous, he went through a thorough questioning process in new circumstances, which he never avoided; renowned, true modesty was a genuine part of his real personality. Simplicity–complex, questioning–was a personality trait that he developed in himself because he knew it was essential for the new men and women who he knew were essential and for whose education he provided concrete elements. Curiosity, humor and intellectual boldness were in him innate.

He never feared change. Quite the contrary, he always demanded it. He maintained that for a process of change–personal, social–to be real, it must always be incomplete, it must continue being and never be permanently finished.

Have I left out anything important? Well, he wrote books. Many of them he actually spoke, that is, they were written based on the transcription of his conversations with friends. He said he was the son of an oral culture, who liked to express himself more in conversation than in writing. But it was also obvious that the challenge of the question, of the contradiction, of the unexpected or newly-formulated idea was exciting for him. For good reason he placed dialogue at the center of his educational conception.

Today I see Paulo as an explorer, amazed by the miracles that his *caminhada* (path) kept leading him to. Let us hope that his life will enrich ours. Let us hope that we don't forget him. And once again, thank you, Brazil.

Esther Pérez
Martin Luther King Memorial Center
Havana, Cuba

Translated into English by Dan Whitesell and Fernando Hernandez
Original Spanish version follows

ESTHER PÉREZ

UN FREIRE A LA HABANERA FREIRE, CUBAN STYLE

Conocí a Paulo Freire en 1987, en lo que algunos considerarían una circunstancia típicamente habanera. Había venido por primera vez a Cuba como invitado especial a un evento, para dictar una conferencia magistral, pero por olvido o equivocación nadie lo fue a esperar al aeropuerto. Un taxista misericordioso lo depositó en un hotel.

Desde allí Paulo hizo lo que muchos otros intelectuales de su generación, varados en circunstancias parecidas, seguramente habían hecho antes que él: buscó en la libreta de teléfonos el de la Casa de las Américas, local del gremio de escritores perdidos, poetas extraviados y ensayistas traspapelados. Le pasaron la llamada a Roberto, quien gritaba para que lo oyeran en Sao Paulo, hasta que entendió que no: Paulo estaba solo en el Hotel Tritón, y quería ayuda para encontrarse con su reunión.

Hechos los trámites del caso y restablecida la comunicación perdida entre invitado e invitantes, a Roberto se le ocurrió que yo debía hacerle una entrevista para publicar en la revista *Casa de las Américas*. Por qué hacer la entrevista era claro: la revista se prestigiaba y era un "palo" periodístico. Después de todo, habíamos sido los primeros en enterarnos de la llegada semiclandestina de Paulo Freire al país. Por qué hacerla yo requiere más explicaciones: la Casa de las Américas intentaba entonces revitalizar su interés en la educación popular, nacido a principios de los años 80, y a mí me habían designado esa misión casi divina, pues su inspirador era Frei Betto, que terminaría por cambiarme la vida, porque a la educación popular acabaría dedicándome a tiempo completo hasta el día de hoy.

Terminamos Paulo Freire, Fernando Martínez y yo comiendo huevos revueltos con jamón en la mesa de mi casa, con una grabadora prestada en la que recogimos la entrevista.

Al final resultó, como a él le gustaba, y como de seguro habría planificado si esas cosas salieran mejor planificadas que naturalmente, un episodio en que forma y contenido se correspondían de manera exacta, o mejor, en que la forma era un metáfora perfecta del contenido. Porque lo cierto es que Paulo Freire era desconocido entre los cubanos, excepto para pequeños grupos que habían tenido la suerte de encontrarse con sus libros editados en el extranjero, o toparse con él, o sus trabajos, o sus seguidores, o su nombre en esta o aquella reunión ocasional.

Volví a encontrarme con Paulo en dos ocasiones. La primera –fugaz– en Brasil, durante su septuagésimo cumpleaños. Era una reunión multitudinaria en la que los invitados íbamos pasando por turno ante la mesa en que estaba sentado, como un mártir enfermo que se somete a los homenajes. La segunda nuevamente en Sao Paulo, en diciembre del año siguiente, y de nuevo, como la primera vez, la ocasión se presentó intermediada, pero ahora más directamente, por Frei Betto. Nos invitó a almorzar a las seis cubanas que habíamos ido a un intercambio con centros brasileños de Educación Popular, y en medio de la conversación nos preguntó si nos gustaría encontrarnos con Paulo. Y allá fuimos, al día siguiente, a su casa, donde esta vez sí conversamos largo con el anciano obviamente frágil, pero lúcido, acerca de su último libro, de su experiencia como Secretario de Educación de Sao Paulo durante el gobierno del Partido de los Trabajadores, del desarrollo de sus ideas después de *Pedagogía de la esperanza* y de su próximo viaje a Cuba –el segundo, el que nunca llegaría a realizar– en mayo de 1997.

Fue él quien mencionó su entrevista habanera y me pidió que le enviara una copia, porque había perdido la suya en una mudanza. Me dijo que la necesitaba porque sentía que ahí había expresado por primera vez intuiciones que maduraron después en sus trabajos de los 90. Nunca se la mandé porque no se presentó la oportunidad, y, como estaba convencida de verlo en La Habana unos meses después, decidí que entregársela personalmente era una buena excusa para que volviéramos a conversar. Murió dos días antes de la fecha programada de su segunda visita a Cuba. Con su muerte, el Brasil intelectual y el Brasil popular perdían, en el lapso de un año, al segundo de dos adelantados, de dos sabios de nuestros tiempos, de dos fundadores de ciencia y conciencia latinoamericanas para el mundo. Paulo Freire se hermanaba también de esta manera con Darcy Ribeiro.

De entonces acá he releído varias veces aquella entrevista de 1988 en busca de lo que Paulo hubiera querido reencontrar en ella, y creo que sé de qué se trata. A partir de la explicación de la idea de la politicidad de la educación, presente en sus reflexiones desde el inicio mismo con *La educación como práctica de la libertad*, revisa allí su vinculación con diferentes procesos revolucionarios contemporáneos (Guinea-Bissau, Granada, Nicaragua...) y su militancia en el Partido de los Trabajadores. Para él esto no se daba por fuera, junto a su práctica de educador, sino que formaba parte de la masa de la misma. De aquí que las reflexiones en torno a la pedagogía dialógica se mezclen, como se mezclan en la vida, con sus visiones acerca de la política. Aparece en la entrevista, de cuerpo entero, el Paulo Freire maduro, que piensa su práctica de pedagogo revolucionario, como él gustaba de definirse, de manera integradora.

Pero más allá de los recuerdos personales –los que lo tratamos o leímos nos hemos reunido ya para intercambiar recuerdos–, es necesario decir algo sobre Paulo para los que no lo conocieron, los que no lo conocen aún, los que lo van a conocer algún día en *Pedagogía del oprimido* o *Cartas desde Guinea-Bissau*.

¿Cómo responder a la pregunta de quién era en definitiva Paulo Freire, de por qué merece homenajes, recordaciones, rencuentros? Era, en primer lugar un intelectual revolucionario latinoamericano, un pensador social y no un reformador de la escuela, papel al que algunos lo quieren reducir. Lo era desde sus primeros escritos, de los ¿lejanos? 60, que sus críticos tildaron de idealistas, con calificativo que él quizás demasiado generosamente recogió y convirtió en motivo de intros-pección y autocrítica. Lo era porque hizo de la socialización de sus descubrimientos un momento tan importante como los propios descubrimientos. Fue una inspiración, para muchos, por diversas razones. Me gustaría resaltar las que en mi caso resultan más movilizadoras.

En primer lugar, Paulo Freire reivindicó la condición intelectual y sus funciones específicas, la importancia de pensar en y para los procesos revolucionarios. Y fue consecuente con esa opción en medio de críticas e incomprensiones, con una coherencia que le duró hasta el final de la vida. Para que hubiera nueva sociedad tenía que haber –dijo y sostuvo con su vida– un pensamiento sobre la misma, que *forma parte* de la praxis. Partir de la práctica y reflexionarla para volver a una práctica transformada fue una de sus ideas centrales. Y la educación podía ser un vehículo privilegiado para que más y más personas se sumaran a esa práctica de acción y pensamiento que postuló y vivió.

En segundo término, sentó las bases de una manera de pensar lo educativo que, siendo específicamente latinoamericana –dado que parte del análisis de la escuela y los procesos de aprendizaje como se dan en la América Latina que conoció–, se abre al mundo como un aporte del continente. Su pedagogía dialógica forma parte de las contribuciones intelectuales de los latinoamericanos a la humanidad y Paulo tuvo, además, el privilegio de hacer su aporte personal en otros ámbitos, notablemente en África.

En tercer lugar, colocó sus reflexiones en un lugar crucial: el de la necesaria refundación de la política para que trascienda los límites de la gobernabilidad y se convierta en el terreno de confluencia de lo público y lo privado, lo racional y lo afectivo, lo humano integral, el de la complejidad enorme que tiene que tener ya un pensamiento liberador para poder ser viable y atractivo. Esta comprensión inicialya en sus primeros libros hablaba de pedagogía liberadora–, temprana en su caso y, por eso, fuente de críticas en su momento, se ha revelado con el paso de los años como uno de los centros del necesario repensamiento de la política, nudo problemático al que las revoluciones y demás prácticas políticas de izquierda del siglo XXI tendrán que enfrentarse en toda su dimensión. En su entrevista habanera tocaba el tema.

Además, echó los cimientos de una pedagogía popular que, por serlo de manera genuina y profunda, fue siempre antidogmática y antisectaria, abierta a todos los aportes, consciente del antagónico, pero intrínsecamente abierta a la contribución del diferente, incluso basada sobre esa contribución, dispuesta a la curiosidad, el riesgo y el cambio permanentes. Pero no absolutizaba sus descubrimientos. Decía que los aportes de la pedagogía anterior tenían que ser comidos, metabolizados, incorporados en nuestra propia práctica pedagógica, porque era sobre esos hombros, y no sobre la nada, que nos alzábamos.

Sabía que sólo la praxis social y política es creadora de personas totales, que no existe la transmisión de valores, sino su creación y recreación por cada generación. Esta tiene que forjarlos en la práctica y la lucha propias, igual y diferente, superadora de las de las generaciones anteriores.

Al hablar de su vida en ocasión de su muerte, muchos han alabado su coherencia. Y es cierto: fue coherente con las verdades que iba descubriendo, con los procesos sociales y políticos en los cuales colaboró, aunque a veces lo hiciera en la discrepancia fraterna; con el movimiento de educación popular, que lo proclamó su inspiración intelectual, y con el que siempre mantuvo una discusión intensa y cariñosa. Quiero resaltar, sin embargo, otra manifestación de su coherencia que me parece de la mayor importancia. Me refiero a la que mantuvo entre sus posiciones intelectuales y su proyecto de vida.

Convencido de su opción por lo popular, se dejó interrogar a fondo por el pueblo latinoamericano sin ceder nunca a las tentaciones del facilismo o la puerilidad. Su indagación fue siempre múltiple, fina, profunda.

Consciente de la necesidad de desarrollo integral de los seres humanos para que seamos capaces de fundar la política sobre bases nuevas, se cinceló el carácter y la actuación con cuidado excepcional. Culto, fue capaz de conversar con todos sin jamás ser condescendiente; famoso, se dejaba interrogar a fondo por las circunstancias nuevas, que nunca evitaba; reconocido, la modestia verdadera formaba parte verdadera de su verdadera personalidad. La sencillez –compleja, problematizadora– fue un rasgo de su personalidad que cultivó porque lo sabía indispensable para los hombres y las mujeres nuevos que sabía imprescindibles y a cuya formación aportó elementos concretos. La curiosidad, el humor y la osadía intelectual le eran consustanciales.

Nunca temió al cambio. Al contrario, lo reivindicó siempre. Sostenía que para que un proceso de cambios –personal, social—
sea verdadero, tiene que estar siempre inacabado, tiene que seguir siendo y nunca ser definitivamente.

¿Algo más que parezca imprescindible? Pues que escribió libros. Muchos de ellos en realidad los habló, es decir. fueron producidos a partir de la transcripción de sus conversaciones con amigos. Decía que era hijo de una cultura oral, que gustaba más de expresarse en la conversación que en la escritura. Pero también era obvio que la provocación de la pregunta, de la contradicción, de la idea inesperada o formulada de otra manera le resultaba una incitación apasionante. No en balde hizo del diálogo el centro de su concepción educativa.

Hoy me represento a Paulo como un explorador asombrado de las maravillas que su *caminhada* le iba proporcionando. Ojalá que su vida sea alimento de la nuestra. Ojalá que no lo olvidemos. Y gracias de nuevo, Brasil.

Esther Pérez
Martin Luther King Memorial Center
Havana, Cuba

LUIS FUENTES

30. REMEMBERING PAULO

Stories

DURING HIS VISIT TO GUINEA-BISSAU

When Paulo Freire arrived in Guinea-Bissau, someone had pointed out to him that the man orating on the street corner in a language other than Portuguese (Creole) was the newly elected president. The crowd was cheering him. Freire knew that the president as well as other elitists were elected in Portugal and spoke Portuguese among themselves. They seemed to look down on their own Creole language.

Paulo and the educator groups that hosted him were more interested in preserving by lexicon the language most spoken throughout the country.[1] They had a very small budget to operate with. Paulo suggested that they use it to buy tape recorders and tapes to document their language as much as possible.

On the day Paulo was leaving to return to Switzerland and the World Council of Churches, the government-controlled newspaper declared: *"The Portuguese language is the most beautiful thing Portugal has given us."*

It appeared that the elite were insulting the group that favored empowering the people via their own language. The irony is that the president was elected by virtue of the votes he won by using it.

PAULO FREIRE AND THE YOUNG LORDS

The Young Lords, whom Paulo had joined at the 116th Street Protestant Church in East Harlem, had congregated to plan their next move two days after taking over the church. They were a Puerto Rican activist civil rights group in the 1960s and 70s who were tired of the lack of city attention to the needs of the community, so they planned to distribute food and clothing and other services from the church.

The media covered this event in numbers, and in many instances did not applaud the action of this group. Paulo saw it as an expression that conveyed the frustrations of a significant element of New York City's Puerto Rican population, who had left the Island due to poor economic conditions. He said:

> These people want justice for themselves and/or the island inhabitants of this American possession. I respect them because they are working in the best interests of an oppressed colony. In Brazil some of our brightest young people are in jail or dead for opposing an unjust military government.[2]

T. Wilson, P. Park and A. Colón-Muñiz (eds.), Memories of Paulo, 133–135.

SILENCE HAS ITS PLACE

In the Chicago audience, activists from all around the U.S.A. waited attentively to hear from the invited guest, Paulo Freire. On this occasion he was to provide answers to their problems. Although to their obvious annoyance, minutes passed by, but he did not speak. Finally, a bearded young Mexican lad stood up and said in Spanish:

"What are you waiting for?". To which Paulo responded, also in Spanish, "Thank you, I was waiting to hear a language we should use!"

He then continued in English.

You are all here because you want answers to your problems. I believe that through praxis we can indeed leave here today with some possible solutions to your problems. First, we must identify the problem, and then with the input of others, seek possible solutions. I personally do not have the solutions to your problems. Let us listen to each other with open minds and the keen sense of justice we already have; speaking in English or Spanish, whatever your chosen language. There are many translators among us.

A young Latino stood up and said: "I am preparing to be a teacher and participating in a bilingual-bicultural program. I can accept a person becoming bilingual, but can a person have two cultures?" Another person from the audience went to the blackboard took a piece of chalk and wrote "Can a person be bicultural?" In addition, others presented their concerns and before long, eight or ten issues were on the board. Then, several voices said, "Let's break into groups around each of these issues", and Paulo then said, "Great, get into a group and when you return from lunch we can share your findings."

He visited each group and contributed where he could. After lunch, each group shared their group's reactions to the issue they had selected. Paulo made comments and contributions to the discussion. After the last report, Freire wrapped it up by saying, "Thank you for a great learning experience and a demonstration of leadership."

MARX, ZINN, CHOMSKY AND FREIRE

Paulo said he slept with a copy of "Das Kapital" under his pillow. He read from it daily like one can suppose the Pope reads from the Bible. He said he was luck to find a copy that was not so bulky.

Although he was captivated by the words of Karl Marx, he additionally read the works of Howard Zinn, from Boston University. Like Zinn, Paulo believed that "you can't be neutral on a moving train." Furthermore, like Zinn and Noam Chomsky of MIT, Paulo wanted students prepared to relinquish the safety of silence and so speak up against injustices wherever they saw them.

However, under military reign as it was in Brazil in the 1960s, telling people to speak up constituted a recipe for trouble. Paulo was considered a threat, resulting in his exile from Brazil. He found refuge in Switzerland, and at the World Council of Churches. He wrote *Pedagogy of the Oppressed* and campaigned internationally against oppression. I remember that in his lectures and writings, Paulo never told the oppressed to take up arms, but rather to secure the power of the vote and to speak up.

NOTES

[1] Although there were many other languages, Creole was popular because it was an Africanized Portuguese, infused by many of the other local languages, but it did not have a written form. Paulo was to help them establish a literacy campaign.

[2] As retold by Paulo, circa 1969

REFERENCES

Cartas a Guine-Bissau: Registros de uma experiencia em processo, Paz e Terra, 1977, translation by Carman St. John Hunter published as *Pedagogy in Process: The Letters to Guinea-Bissau*, Seabury, 1978.

Lubasch, A. H. (1969, December 30). Young lords give food and care at Seized Church. *New York Times, 30*.

Zinn, H. (2002). *You can't be neutral on a moving train: A personal history of our times*. Boston: Beacon Press.

Luis Fuentes, Professor Emeritus
Graduate School of Education
University of Massachusetts, Amherst

FROM THE 1990s

And Afterward

Pia Wong

Suzanne SooHoo

Hermán S. García

Don Cardinal

Mary Poplin

Ana L. Cruz

Karen Cardiero-Kaplan

PIA WONG

31. IN MEMORY OF PAULO FREIRE

With Gratitude and Admiration

"Paulo Freire is now the Secretary of Education for the city of São Paulo…you <u>will</u> do something related to his work there." Martin Carnoy, my doctoral advisor and mentor, began one of my first advising sessions in 1989 with this statement. At first, the possibility boggled my mind. How could I study, much less critique, the work of this person that I admired so much and whose ideas and words had impacted my own life and work so deeply? As a scholar just getting started in the field of international development education, I felt almost incapable of conceptualizing a research question that would be worthy of pursuing within the context of an educational project developed by Paulo Freire. As an activist that was still trying to come to terms with the very fact of being in a Ph.D. program, I also wondered whether I should have been trying to be a contributor to this educational transformation rather than a researcher merely studying Paulo Freire's new initiatives in São Paulo. Shortly after this conversation with Martin, I found myself driving him and his long-time friend, Paulo Freire, from Palo Alto to San Francisco in my tiny Toyota Tercel, addressing these very concerns in depth.

By this time, I had a clearer idea (after much advising from Martin) about the focus of my doctoral research (implementation of the Interdisciplinary Project, the São Paulo precursor to the Citizen School currently in operation in other Brazilian cities, including Porto Alegre). But the other reservations still remained. I can still see Martin hunched in the marginal backseat and Paulo in the front seat saying, "Pia…it is essential that we engage in praxis. We have a truly beautiful educational project. But your research can help us to reflect critically on our work and to understand how to make it more powerful. You are a serious scholar, you will conduct your research responsibly and we will all learn from it. Come to São Paulo and we will help you get your research started." Our conversation turned to other topics and we eventually made it to San Francisco safely!

For the next seven years, I saw Paulo and usually Nita as well, about every two years with occasional phone calls and letters in between. In 1990 I went to São Paulo for one month to conduct pilot research on the Interdisciplinary Project. Paulo and Nita graciously hosted me at several lunches and I met with Ana Maria Saul and other members of Paulo's cabinet to iron out the details of the pilot study. In 1991, I attended a birthday celebration for Paulo's 70th birthday in New York City. I was able to assist with some translations at this event and we squeezed in a brief coffee during the crush of countless well-wishers and admirers. In 1992,

T. Wilson, P. Park and A. Colón-Muñiz (eds.), Memories of Paulo, 139–141.
© 2010 Sense Publishers. All Rights Reserved.

I returned to São Paulo for seven months to conduct research on seven schools implementing the Interdisciplinary Project. During this period, Paulo helped me to meet a cadre of truly amazing "pedagogic militants" (in the words of one of them, Gouvêa), whose knowledge, energy and commitment to the public, popular school was inspiring. Paulo, Nita and I, along with colleagues from Sacramento State, shared a memorable breakfast in Omaha, Nebraska, during the 1996 Pedagogy of the Oppressed Conference there. I saw Paulo for the last time in São Paulo later that year.

It is difficult to put into words the many emotions that my experiences with Paulo Freire evoke, limited though they were. I still marvel at his remarkable humility. He was never arrogant and, though he was sure of his ideas and theories, he seemed always open to listening to those espoused by other people, even by young scholars like myself who had read comparably little and experienced even less. He stood by his invitation at our first meeting and consistently asked me to share my impressions and observations from the school visits I conducted in São Paulo, following up with questions about Interdisciplinary Project successes that I recounted, making notes of instances where teachers working on the Project expressed confusion or frustration to me. I am still moved and inspired by his expansive humanity. He engaged with people with great love and honesty but at the same time always expected the most of them. I remember once during a question and answer session after a lecture, he was asked to be more explicit about how the ideas in *Pedagogy of the Oppressed* could be converted into a viable project for a particular group in the U.S. He responded that while he was excited by the group's objectives, they needed to engage in their own struggle to make sense of those ideas in their particular context. He added that though such work was difficult and challenging, they had the capacity to do it and could not achieve success in their project without such a struggle.

I wrote and talked with Paulo many times about the ways in which he shaped my professional and personal development, but my gratitude is worth recounting here, particularly for the sake of Nita and his family. I read *Pedagogy of the Oppressed* before I met Paulo. It was a book that had a powerful effect on me, helping me to translate my own naïve but passionate commitments to social change into clear and operationable ideas. After reading that book, I read everything I could find by Freire and I tried, clumsily, to put some of his ideas into practice as a community development staff person for the City of Oakland and during a brief summer school teaching stint with junior high school students in the Portrero Hill/Hunter's Point neighborhoods in San Francisco. The Interdisciplinary Project, conceptualized by Freire and operationalized by a group of educators that were smart, thoughtful, courageous, creative and hard-working, is the vision of democratic, liberatory education that gives me hope in my most cynical and discouraged moments. I begin all of my classes in our teacher preparation program with an in-depth description of the Interdisciplinary Project and its more current iterations (the Citizen School in Porto Alegre, for example) so that new generations of teachers can know that "another world is possible." In an introductory course on critical pedagogy for our M.A. program, we read *Pedagogy of the Oppressed* and discuss and debate the ideas Paulo espoused. Each semester there is at least one student–often one of our Latina students from a migrant farm worker family or a Black student from the Bay Area or a teacher with working class roots–who will approach me and say, "This book speaks so deeply to me. This IS my experience." Paulo's work in Brazil–from the cultural circles in the late 1950's/early 1960's to the Interdisciplinary Project in the early 1990's–orients the work that I have done for the last six years in conjunction with teacher and faculty colleagues in the Equity Network who are committed to improving the education of low income and culturally and linguistically diverse students in Sacramento and the teachers who teach them. And lastly, through Paulo, I have met many people in Brazil and in the U.S. that I now count among my dearest friends and most valued colleagues, thus forming a collaborative that supports each of us to pursue a vision of democratic education and social transformation that, like Paulo, we all share.

I feel blessed to have been a small part of Paulo's life and to have had the opportunity to experience the power of his democratic educational vision. Paulo Freire–você é um amigo que está dentro da minha coração sempre, cujas ideias poderosas e radicais guiam para sempre o meus pensamentos e as minhas ações. (Paulo Freire–you are a friend that I carry deep in my heart; your powerful and radical ideas will forever guide my thoughts and actions.)

Com muita admiração e profundo carinho para sempre….Pia

Pia Wong
Professor, Bilingual/Multicultural Education Department
Sacramento State University, California

SUZANNE SOOHOO

32. PAULO

I Am Here

When hungry, I eat.
When tired, I sleep.
I'm here.
(Zen quote)

In my early adolescent years, my Chinese father introduced me to a Zen world view. One lesson was to live in the moment: When one is hungry, one eats. When one is tired, one sleeps. When one is rested, one gets up. No need for an alarm clock, I remembered thinking. But the point is not simply to listen to the universe; it is also to be wholly present, attentive, and humbled by all that surrounds us. This stance is informed by a deep respect for others and all of life's activities. It allows me to be present both here and now wherever life brings me.

Paulo Freire embraced a similar stance. Authors in this collection have written about how Paulo's work has influenced them. I write instead about two consciousness awakening incidents with Paulo in person. I remember at the University of California in Irvine in the late 1980s after Paulo's keynote, standing in a long line, waiting to talk with him. Among the throngs of admirers anxiously waiting to hold court with this legendary educator and philosopher, I was nervous and uncertain about his reaction to my potential question. I was an elementary school principal who was accustomed to reading only executive briefs and a new doctoral student cutting her teeth on *Pedagogy of the Oppressed*, trying desperately to get through chapter 3 and definitely unworthy to speak to Paulo Freire. When I got to the front of the line, to my surprise, Paulo listened to me as if he had all the time in the world, as if we were the only two people in the room. He made everything else vanish.

I complimented him on his work and then asked *that* question that everyone has asked him either directly or silently, "Why is the language you use in your books so hard for me to understand?" Hegemony, conscientization, praxis–concepts so foreign to my notions of schooling and learning, words that made me feel inadequate and "outside of the club." It wasn't Paulo's Portuguese accent that discomforted me; it was his esoteric academic language. I recounted that he, Henry Giroux, Stanley Aronowitz, and Peter McLaren all seemingly spoke the same language and I confessed that I understood little of what they wrote.

Instead of answering me, Paulo asked, "Suzanne, tell me what you do when a new child comes to your second grade classroom, speaking another language? What do you do?" I answered, "I try to regard all the resources s/he brings to the

T. Wilson, P. Park and A. Colón-Muñiz (eds.), Memories of Paulo, 143–144.
© *2010 Sense Publishers. All Rights Reserved.*

class; culture, language, ancestry as rich gifts to enhance our classroom and our literacy." Paulo inquired, "Then why will you not accept those critical theorists (Giroux, Aronowitz, and McLaren) in the language they speak?"

Paralyzed by his response, a growing realization moved through my body–I had privileged my need to understand over the language of their science. Behind my request was an expectation that they speak my language, an insistence that they had an obligation to talk and write in a manner that would accommodate me.

In a fatherly way, Paulo held a mirror up to me and in it, I saw an elitist. My responsibility became self evident–I must learn their language so that I may understand and fully appreciate them and their ideas. This was an opportunity for me to "learn without mastery" (Hooks, 1994).

I was humbled both by this realization and by the graceful pedagogy Paulo unveiled in front of me–reminding me that it wasn't all about me, yet gifting me with this teachable moment and his full attention. Thank you, Paulo, for being there for me.

In a second encounter with Paulo, my colleague, Tom Wilson and I were event coordinators for an event featuring Paulo. Paulo was late for his talk. I became worried, anxious as I watched the room fill with people, breaking out into an unflattering sweat. We went to look for him. I frantically rang the doorbell of the faculty house and no one answered. We raced around back to the patio sliding glass door. The drapes were pulled so we saw nothing. I desperately tugged on the door handle. The door flew across the track and we suddenly see Paulo with his wife, Nita, sitting on his lap, kissing and tenderly caressing her. I stopped in my tracks, speechless, consumed with a cacophony of conflicting thoughts, feelings and emotions–embarrassment, surprise, relief... In contrast, Paulo in a calm, confident and reassuring tone, said to us, "Tom, Suzanne, I am here."

Paulo was nonplussed and another "aha" moment uncovered itself to me. Questions ran through my mind: Why are you here and not there (at the keynote podium)? Why are you kissing your wife now and not later? And more importantly, why am I uncomfortable with this display of love? What Puritanical values stole my voice and censured my appreciation for sensuality?

There was no artificial barrier between Paulo's professional and personal lives; both melded together to form a passionate, intelligent human being. Years later, when he and Donaldo Macedo spoke of a pedagogy of love, I understood love as respect, courage, humility and something deeply personal. Love means being totally present (as Paulo was for his wife and for us students), wholly committed, and truly humble. With careful deliberation, I summon this love into my daily being. To my dear father and Paulo, as a daughter, teacher, and activist, thank you for helping me to get to the **here** and now.

Suzanne SooHoo, Professor
College of Educational Studies
Chapman University, California

HERMÁN S. GARCÍA

33. WAYS I GOT TO KNOW PAULO FREIRE

My acquaintance with Paulo Freire was through his writings. His work has been so inspirational for me throughout my entire academic career and more so today. I can't imagine talking about teaching and social justice without invoking Paulo Freire's pedagogical legacy. I read *Pedagogy of the Oppressed* in 1973 in my undergraduate years as part of a specialization in a Chicano Studies class. Paulo's thought-provoking writings were a challenge for me as an undergraduate, yet I could connect with the spirit of his theoretical framework. It was in Paulo's works where I connected to the various critical perspectives he offered across his writings.

Paulo Freire was a down-to-earth connection for me because his writings reflected the "everyday" of people's lives while framing his pedagogy within a theoretically constructivist approach that served not only educators and students, but whole communities. His works broadened my thinking about what learning might be, how it might emerge, and how I could engage with students and attempt to have a transformative effect on their lives, on the lives of educator colleagues, and on communities at large. Paulo, through his writings, taught me that the cultural politics of learning was central to understanding issues of power across sites of struggle which needed to be negotiated. Paulo's human warmth came across in all of his works He never had a selfish motive underlying what he wrote. His writings were clearly intended to be studied in context of where one lived, worked and struggled and taken up according to the local context and conditions.

The concept of emancipation comes to mind for me when I think of Paulo Freire. I was quite fortunate to have visited the Paulo Freire Institute in São Paulo, Brazil in 1999 shortly after Paulo had passed. Upon entering the Paulo Freire Institute, I quickly sensed the magnitude of his persona among his native populace with whom he had made his life and the library of materials he had studied and collected. There was a sensation for me that he was still alive and it made me painfully aware of how a person of his stature could actually be gone. Years earlier, I had met Donaldo Macedo and through him I met Henry Giroux and Peter McLaren. They also spoke warmly of Paulo Freire, as they knew him personally and had worked with him closely, especially Donaldo. I knew, through their descriptions, that Paulo was a very special person, the kind of human being that we rarely get to connect with in our lives. Nonetheless, I had connected with Paulo's human character a quarter of a century earlier in a Chicano Studies course as an under-graduate.

As a result of a TESOL Master's degree program that NMSU offered in Brazil from 1999–2002, I studied and learned Portuguese at a high intermediate level. Over the years, I have read in Portuguese and listened to Paulo in Portuguese on

T. Wilson, P. Park and A. Colón-Muñiz (eds.), Memories of Paulo, 145–147.

various topics on tapes, videos, DVDs and other formats in which his activist discourse and pedagogy took me to his advocacy spirit, the essence of him. As a result of learning Portuguese language and Brazilian culture, I also learned that there is a unique word in Portuguese that doesn't exist in Spanish or English that the Brazilians use, *saudade*. It means the profound feeling of missing someone or something with the hope of seeing that someone again, although unlikely. Hardly any other language in the world has a word with such deep meaning, making *saudade* a distinct mark of the Portuguese language. It has been stated that this, more than anything else, represents what it means to be Brazilian. I realize Paulo will never return, but I also know his spirit lives within us in many different ways. That is how I feel about Paulo Freire when I talk about him and his works in my classes. It is as if we hung out. And, in a figurative kind of way, we did: I hung out in his readings and got to know him through those readings in deeper ways than if I had hung around him in person. It was in his writings where Paulo revealed his spirit, the essence of his revolutionary heart. And it was through his writings that he let you into his very being, his non-stop revolutionary mindedness.

Paulo's revolutionary spirit is alive in his writing. One can easily detect his heartfelt notion of emancipatory and transformative struggle. He seemed to always be in avant-garde gear by struggling for an improved difference for the underdog. He was willing, as he demonstrated many times in his life, to give it his all, although it was quite costly to him and his family over the years. Not many of us can say that, at least not in the way Paulo Freire could say it. And for that sacrifice, I am grateful to Paulo. I really think that was the nature of his being and no one, no government, no ideology, was going to change that in Paulo Freire. I don't think *he* could change it if he wanted to. It was born in him and grew stronger as he got older.

I believe Paulo was a patient person. It seems to me that only a very patient person could endure the struggles that he not only endured, but survived. In his writings he made a statement that we had to be impatiently patient. When I think of revolution, it conveys an immediate notion of action, something that needs to be done now. Yet in Paulo's logic of revolution, I see the unfathomable power of his belief of struggling impatiently patient, and I come to the realization that revolution is a journey, not a destination. It seems to me also that in his approach to revolution as a way of life, he had no recipes or formulas. Revolution meant what the people struggling wanted it to mean, for better or for worse. Paulo Freire's notion of struggle was an actionable journey, not a concluding destination.

Paulo gave us, certainly gave me, such a rich vocabulary and theoretical framework from where to launch my pedagogies. Theory and practice combined became *praxis*, a truly Freirian concept. Clearly, it was much more than theory and practice because there was pedagogy, politics, power, love, community and more. From this framework was conceived critical pedagogy, a major revolutionary undertaking in pedagogical circles around the globe. For me personally, the multiple themes of critical pedagogy transformed me as an educator. I cannot imagine not being a criticalist in the broadest sense of the term.

Pedagogy and politics à la Paulo Freire provided me with a sense of social and cultural justice. The struggle for social justice in sociopolitical and pedagogical contextual relationships keeps me inspired. I remain evermore grateful to Paulo Freire.

Hermán S. García
Curriculum and Instruction
New Mexico State University, Las Cruces

DON CARDINAL

34. THE RESPONSIBILITY OF PRIVILEGE AND THE KEY TO UNDERSTANDING

Prior to my meeting Paulo, he was like a star baseball player to me. He was reminiscent of a great contemporary player while also being a legend, as if he played with Babe Ruth or Jackie Robinson–maybe even like he *was* Babe Ruth. Being a baseball fan most of my life made this analogy meaningful for me. Even more momentous was knowing I was going to meet him. Not just a quick hello–I was going to spend a full day with him. I felt like a kid with a million questions to ask, all the while knowing I may not be able to articulate any of the questions when the moment came, or at least not to the degree where I would sound even reasonably intelligent. My concern was amplified by the belief that one of my questions may be too personal, too attacking or too rude. In June, 1996, the "Babe" (Paulo) arrived. My first impression was one of surprise. He was not really nine feet tall and thunder didn't really strike after each thing he said. In fact, he was not large in stature at all and he spoke softly, sometimes very softly.

My first chance to ask a question was in a large hall with about 30 people each asking questions to which Paulo would respond. It felt to me like Kahlil Gibran's book, *The Prophet*, where the people of Orphalese would ask the prophet "Speak to us of love or sorrow." But, instead of standing and speaking to the masses from above, Paulo sat, with his head lower than others, looking at the ground often and the people asked, "Speak to us of oppression and liberation." He answered questions as if he were secure with his response, yet willing to discuss other possibilities. Questions continued to come, in a tenor of disciple-to-prophet, apparently motivated by reverence of the audience, not any need or desire of Paulo's. Even though the answers to most of the questions Paulo had written about so many times, Paulo answered each question as if he had just thought of the response, as if it were a tailored response to the specific person. I thought then that Paulo's power came from his unique melding of humility and inner strength–he was not really like Babe Ruth at all–yet oddly similar. I knew there was more time in the day to ask my questions so we continued with the disciple-prophet scenario for the rest of that great event. Paulo did volunteer information at times which I found the most meaningful. After responding to a question about oppression in America, Paulo went on to say, and I paraphrase, "your biggest mistake is that the various cultural/ethnic groups in America do not join together. If they would come together, America could be what it promises to be."

We then went to lunch with Paulo along with maybe six of seven other faculty members. I was seated right across from Paulo, the table was narrow and I felt that if we both leaned forward at the same moment our heads would knock together

T. Wilson, P. Park and A. Colón-Muñiz (eds.), Memories of Paulo, 149–151.

(if they had, I am sure that would be the story I am telling now instead of this one). We were at a small Cuban restaurant near Chapman University and I remember we ordered the same lunch: beans and rice. I had two overwhelming and overriding emotions. First, I was thinking "how cool was this?" I am sitting so close to Paulo and I could ask him anything I want. We could talk about the weather, politics, how his plane flight went, or... Then it hit me, the other overriding emotion! This was the ideal time to ask the questions I had waited to ask for a long time. Shall I ask the academic questions, or is it time to ask the tough question I feared would be too bold? Who was I to put this guy on the spot? He was our guest. No, I said to myself. This is the time to ask and how can one believe in critical inquiry and not ask tough questions. I waited for the beans and rice to come, as if with the food would come courage and clarity. The table conversation was both light and heavy. We talked about his new book, political struggles in Brazil, the weather. Back and forth, from "how's the food," to what he thought about a particular news event in America.

There was a slight pause in the conversation; I think everyone was taking a bite of food at the same time. The words came out of my mouth "Paulo, I have a tough question I would like to ask." He did not appear shaken by my announcement. In fact, he loaded up with another bite of beans and rice and kindly, while chewing said, "Yes, go ahead." All faculty were focused. "So why, when you and other critical theorists write of liberation, do you write in such a coded language that exceeds the reading ability of the oppressed? Isn't that hypocritical," I asked. There, I said it, and there were more where that came from, I thought. For some reason, however, he did not look shaken. In fact, later in the conversation he told me that this was one of the most common questions he receives anywhere he goes around the world. He said his words were to those who were willing to work to understand them. He went on to tell us that it took him two hours, with dictionary in hand, to adequately understand the title of Henry Giroux's new book (who, by the way, he called the best living American educational philosopher. He then corrected himself and said the best living educational philosopher, period). Paulo went on to say that he did not see it as contradictory at all, that the language of critical theorists is complex. He said the ideas are intricate and deserve great attention and study. He concluded, suggesting that the language of critical theory is not restrictive to the oppressed, but rather, the lazy (my word, I forget his). His focus on the hard work of understanding threw me off a little. Almost immediately something turned around in my thinking, disequilibrium may be the best way to phrase it. For the sake of brevity, let me just say that, at that moment, I sensed a decoupling of the equation "literacy equals liberation." I began to recognize my own "intellectual laziness." If a man this smart, this original, has to work so hard to "understand" notions of liberation, who am I to think a single reading of *Pedagogy of the Oppressed* even approximates understanding its notions? Over time, and very careful reading, I began to understand that the ideas of, for example, *conscientization* and *praxis*, concepts I had "read" before, were not stand-alone concepts. I began to question if these were intellectual concepts at all. The process of conscientization, I began to think, could only be fully understood by someone oppressed and certainly not by me, a White man of privilege. The most I could hope for is an intellectual understanding of conscientization, even then, an understanding that would take a lot of hard work. Maybe the most important thing I took away from my day with Paulo was a sense of responsibility of my privilege–that with privilege comes the responsibility to work hard to intellectually understand what others experience.

You meet a lot of people in life, some you forget, some you remember. I remember becoming a little more humble over my beans and rice with Paulo.

Thanks, Paulo, for helping me understand that understanding is hard work.

Don Cardinal
Dean, College of Educational Studies
Chapman University, Orange, California

MARY POPLIN

35. THE MYSTICAL SIDE OF PAULO

I will always remember Paulo as a man with a very big heart. I remember one summer night, we asked him to speak to our new teachers at a dinner. He and Nita came in with the glow of newlyweds. As he began to speak, he spoke about the beauty of the sky and the flowers he had noticed on his way into the building and the love he had for Nita. He told us if he did not acknowledge these things, he would have no right to speak. Then he somehow tied the beauty of the world with the call for justice. I call that his "justice and flowers address." It only lasted about 15 minutes but the lesson was not lost on those of us who heard him.

Then on one of his last visits to campus in 1992, we recorded him for almost two hours (now available on DVD).[1] We employed the Los Angeles Educational Television Network to record two panels of interviews with several faculty, graduates and current graduate students. One graduate, James Astman, an accomplished educator and headmaster of a private school in Los Angeles, asked him the following question:

> You write about education as a fundamentally political enterprise but when I hear you speak now, or when I read what you write, I can't help but [be] impressed by the religious dimension. [Paulo, laughing, interjects, "yes, that is very interesting."] Could you talk about education, not as a political but as a religious enterprise?

> **Paulo**   Yes, that is very interesting. Look, first of all, you have the right to think like this and to understand me like this, it is also an intellectual exercise you did now. And, of course, I also cannot deny, that in my answer, there is something that maybe goes beyond ....for example, a positivist scientist in listening to me now would say, 'Bah, no, it is a crazy person. It's a religious discourse.'

I deny that, look, not because I am against religion, but because even though it has some mystical understanding of my presence in the world, it is also a strongly political speech. It has lots of roots in politics–the things I said before–the duty of transforming, of becoming engaged in a permanent process of transformation. For example, even though there are some religious dimensions in my answer–maybe there is hiding a possible religious, mystical, a certain theology, a theological conception, which does not dichotomize for example, worldliness from transcendence, history from

T. Wilson, P. Park and A. Colón-Muñiz (eds.), Memories of Paulo, 153–155.
© *2010 Sense Publishers. All Rights Reserved.*

meta-history–which tries to grasp the totality and the relationships dialectically between the world and the transcendence. In the last analysis, it is also politics; do you see?

Then, when you ask me, 'Paulo, speak a little bit about education and the religion. I would say that first of all religion is a right of human beings–to be religious or not. And the education vis-à-vis religion should be–we come back to politics again–democratic education. The democratic teachers would put into practice such a kind of education that would have to clarify the right the persons have to believe, or not believe–to make this choice, yes or no.

But, maybe this is not what you would like to believe or to hear from me. Maybe you got the impression that I was becoming more mystical than I was before. I can tell you that I am not interested even in denying my beliefs– what is mystical in this understanding of the world and of my presence here. But I continue to be strongly political man in being an educator. And the political nature of education is very clear for me and continues to be, and I think that we must assume this in order to transform reality.

Anyway, I like your question. This is the first time that I received this question and it is so interesting. From time to time, I am surprised that there is a question I was not expecting. And maybe my wife, who is in the other room looking at me, watching, maybe, because she has experience of seeing me, she is saying, 'this question is a very new question to Paulo, because I am seeing that he is not so fine in the answer.' But the other questions, I see from time to time and I almost have the answer. [laughter] Maybe the next time someone asks this question I will be better. But it is a very good question.

After the videotaping, we went to lunch where Paulo discovered he loved arugula salads. He looked very tired and I said to him, "I hope we did not wear you out." He looked at me very intently and said, "I am just thinking of the religion question, I think I did not give a good answer, I have to think it about it more."

I do not know what happened when he continued to think about the question; perhaps Nita does, but I do know there was something in Paulo that knew the presence of the numinous, the mystical. It seems the flowers, the sky, his deep love for Nita and for Elza, and his suffering made his heart stronger and softer in ways uncommon for those of us who work with critical theory. It made him humble enough to remain open to the possibility that there was always more–more to be learned, more to do, more to love.

I have been twice blessed by getting to know both Paulo and Mother Teresa. Oddly enough, there were some similarities between them besides the fact that they both died within months of one another. Paulo and Mother Teresa both had a very strong, not sweet, heart for the poor, a very determined call to promote justice. Paulo promoted justice through politics, and she through her relationship with Christ.

I remember Paulo saying that sometimes an individual commits what he called "class suicide" and becomes radically transformed. Mother Teresa called this radical transformation "dying to self in order to live more fully"–"becoming empty of ourselves so God could work his justice through us."

Both of them knew that justice requires a sacrifice.

NOTES

[1] The videos can be ordered from the Institute for Education in Transformation, Claremont Graduate University, c/o Professor Mary Poplin, 150 East Tenth, Claremont, CA 91711.

Mary Poplin, Professor of Education
Director of the Institute for Education in Transformation
Claremont Graduate University, California

ANA L. CRUZ

36. PAULO AND ME

A Personal Narrative of Encounters

For me Paulo Freire is more than an intellectual influence; he permeates my way of living. However, I personally never met Paulo Freire. My hope of one day being able to personally discuss with Paulo his ideas and his influence on my work faded away in May of 1997.

INTRODUCTION

Paulo Freire and what he stood for, nevertheless, entered my life quite early. I was born in Manaus, the heart of Amazonas, Brazil. Even though I was raised in a middle-class family, my father a lawyer and my mother a teacher, I was well aware of the poverty that is a part of the fabric of Brazil. I attended a Catholic all-girls High School in Manaus, with students of middle to upper socio-economic back-grounds. My sociology teacher was also a known activist, considered a subversive, even a communist. Many believed that this teacher's ideas, behavior and attitude were a result of her association with people like Paulo Freire. Consequently, many parents and more conservative educators did not see her as a positive influence on us, her students. She introduced me and my classmates to the ideas of Paulo Freire. I was just a young high school student but was fascinated with my teacher's discourse of social equality and the power of education as a means of social transformation. *"Nice to meet you Mr. Paulo Freire; if my teacher draws her ideas about helping the poor, provide more educational opportunities for the miserable and poor to improve their social conditions and participation in society from you, I am sure you will have a lot to teach me!"* These were my thoughts when my teacher asked us students to read and to discuss with her the *Pedagogy of the Oppressed* (Freire, 1970), while Brazil was still under the spell of the military dictatorship. This was how I got to know Paulo Freire. It was a watershed moment for me. What I was exposed to in this Amazonian classroom never left me–it stayed with me for life and was formative in my own career as an educator.

RESEARCHING MUSIC AND DEAFNESS

I re-encountered Paulo Freire at the time of my graduate studies at the University of Tennessee in Knoxville, Tennessee. During the re-encounter I was not a young girl anymore, but a woman who had already considerable teaching experience at

T. Wilson, P. Park and A. Colón-Muñiz (eds.), Memories of Paulo, 157–159.
© 2010 Sense Publishers. All Rights Reserved.

various grade levels. My teaching experience and my graduate studies were allowing me now to better connect theory and praxis, an intrinsic relationship Paulo Freire stressed repeatedly. This mature re-encounter with Freire allowed me to expand the application of his ideas to another educational realm where people are still disenfranchised by the label of "disabled." With a more cognizant understanding of equality and social justice, I researched music and deafness and specifically applied a phenomenological approach to understand how one Deaf individual constructs meaning in music. The issue of some Deaf individuals engaging in music, however, very often brings to light the oppressor-oppressed relationship between those who do not believe that Deaf individuals are "able" to enjoy music and those Deaf individuals who are trying to do so. Deaf individuals can experience music and derive benefits from it through plural pathways (a combination of residual hearing, seeing, feeling, moving, etc.) as opposed to the direct pathway (hearing) (Cruz, 1997). These Deaf individuals have to confront outside pressures (from the normally hearing culture) and inside pressures (from a large segment of the Deaf culture who follow ideological concepts espousing music as an identifier of the normally hearing) of insisting that music is not suitable for the Deaf. In this context, Freire's concept of *conscientização* (critical consciousness) (Freire, 1970, 1973)–representing the development of the awakening of critical awareness–becomes imperative for Deaf individuals to overcome any preconceived notions about their deafness (as a limiting identifier with political and contextual meanings) and their ability to enjoy and engage in musical activities. Paulo Freire was a constant companion on my way to the doctorate.

TEACHING

I have had discussions with many colleagues about the "appropriate" time for introducing Paulo Freire to students. Many are of the belief that Paulo Freire's literary work and ideas are not appropriate for an inexperienced audience, but rather, they are designed for professionals with appropriate intellectual skills, exposure and a very good command of the vocabulary and ideas pertinent to critical pedagogy. It seems that the overall concern is that Freire's work is "too complex" for the novice and only after reaching a certain "academic maturity" one should be allowed to be exposed to Freire's ideas and writings to avoid misunderstanding or no understanding at all.

Now I have the chance to assume the role of my high school sociology teacher and introduce Paulo Freire to another generation of students. In my own classroom at a U.S. community college, I expose teacher education students at the freshman and sophomore level to the world of Paulo Freire. The class material is derived from *Teachers as Cultural Workers* (Freire, 1998). We read selected chapters and discuss the material critically in class. Understanding of the reading assignments might be tough for some students, but group and class discussion and proper guidance can overcome this problem. The goal is to foster critical thinking in the students, to have them ponder social reality, and to make them realize that they–as future teachers–can engage in social change. The students will also reflect upon their values and belief systems and how these can and will influence their teaching. I believe that all teacher education students need to be not only cognizant of Paulo's work, but that they have to get exposure to it early, so they can build upon this foundation. My students, therefore, engage with Paulo in a way similar to the path I took as a high-school student in Manaus. Through my students I continue to constantly revisit and reinvent my own understanding of Paulo's ideas.

LIVING AND ENACTING THE MEMORIES

Despite much time that passed since my first encounter with Paulo in high school, his ideas still strike me as a revolutionary way to face the world! I continue to re-encounter Paulo and stay connected to his work by meeting and communicating with scholars who work, teach and conduct research following the tracks laid down for us by Paulo (e.g., McLaren and Kincheloe, 2007). *The Paulo Freire Special Interest Group* of the American Educational Research Association and, especially, Joe Kincheloe's and Shirley Steinberg's *The Paulo and Nita Freire Project for Critical Pedagogy* are two venues that allow such interaction. At the launch of The Paulo and Nita Freire Project for Critical Pedagogy in Montreal, Canada, I met Nita Freire. Reading Nita's book *Chronicles of Love* (Freire, 2001) and my conversations with her brought Paulo much closer to me. Combining my reading of Paulo's work with the lively descriptions from Nita about the person Paulo was, I am now able to understand him on a more personal level: I finally met Paulo Reglus Neves Freire!

REFERENCES

Cruz, A. (1997). *An examination of how one deaf person constructs meaning in music; A phenomeno-logical perspective* (p. 140). Unpublished Doctoral Dissertation, University of Tennessee.
Freire, A. M. A. (2001). *Chronicles of love: My life with Paulo Freire* (p. 168). New York: Peter Lang.
Freire, P. (1970). *Pedagogy of the oppressed* (p. 164). New York: Continuum.
Freire, P. (1973). *Education for critical consciousness* (p. 146). New York: Seabury Press.
Freire, P. (1998). *Teachers as cultural workers: Letters to those who dare teach* (p. 100). Boulder, CO: Westview Press.
McLaren, P., & Kincheloe, J. L. (Eds.). (2007). *Critical pedagogy: Where are we now?* (p. 411). New York: Peter Lang.

Ana Cruz, Professor of Education
St. Louis Community College .St. Louis, Missouri

KAREN CADIERO-KAPLAN

37. NAMING THE WORLD AND BECOMING A BEING IN THE WORLD

One Teacher's Journey on the Path of Empowerment

Paulo Freire, more than any other scholar, both modeled and taught me that, as teachers, we must "educate the curiosity through which knowledge is constituted as it grows and refines itself through the very existence of knowing." (*Pedagogy of the Heart*, p. 31) That is the fact that we–teachers, students, citizens–as knowing beings in the world, have the ability to engage in the process of knowledge creation and production. Freire believed that knowledge resides in everyone and that the critical teacher brings out that knowledge and creates spaces for new knowledge to be learned, critiqued and generated.

While I never personally heard Paulo Freire speak, his words and his work have influenced me in my daily role of advocating for student and teacher voice throughout my career as an educator. Paulo's message first impacted me as a special education teacher and continues to this day as I now reside at the university as a professor in education. Paulo Freire's influence on me has grown as I have grown, due to my early experiences reading and working with professors and colleagues who brought his writings alive for me through their work and actions, including Rene Nuñez, Alberto Ochoa, Antonia Darder, Peter McLaren and Donaldo Macedo. By putting Paulo's words into action, these wonderful professors provided me the opportunity to go further in my education and work than I ever could have imagined. I am here today writing about my connections to a person I consider my mentor and model for teaching who stated that educational practice should not be "restricted" to a "reading of the word," a "reading of text," but rather believing that it should also include a "reading of context," a "reading of the world." (*Pedagogy of the Heart*, p. 43)

In my early years of teaching elementary urban adolescents with *special needs* I was told that I expected too much of my students, that I was too idealistic and had to realize their realities of being poor with uneducated parents was a "problem" with few solutions or a "deficit" that had to be addressed. One administrator even told me "every young teacher begins idealistically, Karen, but eventually, they, like you, learn to deal with reality." The reality she referred to was the assumption that these children had little opportunity to succeed in society and that the best we could do was teach them the appropriate social skills and sufficient academics to function in low-skill jobs. These statements, rather than deter me, only reaffirmed my commitment to my ideals that every child carries potential and deserves to be engaged in the world and in their education. It was my responsibility to learn from

T. Wilson, P. Park and A. Colón-Muñiz (eds.), Memories of Paulo, 161–163.

these children and take them from where they entered and provide them with experiences that would engage their hearts and minds. I was committed to teaching my students in a humanizing and respectful manner, always looking for what strengths, abilities and knowledge they brought with them, rather than focusing on what they lacked.

While I carried this strong belief in my students and myself, I often felt isolated and misunderstood by those around me. My administrators, staff developers, and peers placated me when I asked many questions of why certain methods of teaching were utilized or valued over others, and how students were placed, labeled and many times segregated. The responses I received were "you ask too many questions," "you just need to follow the district mandate as set out" or "don't rock the boat."

Then, in my graduate studies, I came to read *Pedagogy of the Oppressed*, and for the first time I felt my ideas and way of approaching my work in the classroom were validated. Through this book and the dialogue that ensued in the reading, I was finally given the key to understanding my struggles. I was provided with the words to express what I had experienced, felt and known for so long. First, Paulo gave me the words to name the "banking model" of education and to understand the rationale for this approach. Most importantly, he helped me to understand the politicized nature of education. I saw, through Freire's words, that I, as teacher, was a hand-maiden of the oppressor via my compliance with the system, and saw that it was possible to challenge the status quo, especially for my students labeled "learning disabled" and "severely emotionally disturbed." Through readings and critical dialogue of Paulo's work, I developed a language of resistance for my students and myself. I see this as the language of possibility and hope.

It was through the writings of Paulo Freire that I began to find answers to my questions and reasons for the actions taken by the system to "choose certain methods and curriculum." For the first time in my career, I felt I had the right and responsibility to learn more and question more, and realized that "education is an act of love, and thus an act of courage." (*Education for Critical Consciousness*, p. 38) I now had the courage to stand up for my students and myself, knowing that it was my duty as an educator to advocate for social justice. From this point on I was able to distinguish between a "naïve consciousness" and a "critical consciousness." I could now name myself as a critical and progressive educator, labels I had not heard before, but now recognized and owned. These ideas of critical pedagogy provided the words to name my ideology and practice. Freire was a role model for me, and his work in developing literacy programs in Brazil taught me that one could be a scholar and human being in the world, a human being that was able to walk in the academy, as well as the streets, to lead from the heart and the mind in order to advocate for the oppressed, using education as the tool for self-advocacy, empowerment and liberation. Paulo Freire provided the words to name the world by linking my reading of the world to empowering words and defining phrases of democratic thinking and actions.

While it may seem I write from the past, this past informs my present work in teacher education and as a policy leader for English learners. Every summer I re-read *Pedagogy of the Oppressed* and *Pedagogy of the Heart*, and throughout the school year I revisit other writings, as I engage critical questions and seek words of challenge, wisdom, hope, or inspiration. Recently, in working with policy makers in my state, I had a few months where I felt that it might not be worthwhile to continue with the work of engaging the conservative agenda that seemed to have a stranglehold on the work for which I was engaged. As I contemplated walking away, I picked up *Pedagogy of Hope* and as I usually do; I just randomly opened the book, looked down, and I came upon these words, reading them as if Paulo was speaking directly to me, he stated:

> One of the tasks of the progressive educator, through a serious, correct political analysis, is to unveil opportunities for hope, no matter what the obstacle may be. After all, without hope there is little we can do. It will be hard to struggle on, and when we fight as hopeless or despairing persons, our struggle will be suicidal. (p. 9).

I put down the book and realized in that moment I had to stay in the struggle and now a year later, I am glad I did. For we are making progress and moving forward, but change is slow and the work for democratic ideals is constant.

I am thankful that Paulo Freire entered my life and my world via texts and scholars who not only knew him personally, but also brought his words and work to life in their own teaching, learning and writing. I now do that for my students and in my work and realize that this man from Brazil and of the world has left a legacy that can only make the world a better place. As did Paulo, I believe that:

I am not a being in the life support but a being in the world, with the world and with others; I am a being who makes things, knows and ignores, speaks, fears, and takes risks, dreams and loves, becomes angry and enchanted. (*Pedagogy of the Heart*, pg. 35)

Thus, it is my responsibility to share his words so others can name their worlds and become beings in and with the world.

REFERENCES

Freire, P. (2002). *Education for critical consciousness*. New York: Continuum Publishing.
Freire, P. (2000). *Pedagogy of the heart*. New York: Continuum Publishing.
Freire, P. (1995). *Pedagogy of hope*. New York: Continuum Publishing.

Karen Cadiero-Kaplan, Associate Professor
San Diego State University, California

SHIRLEY R. STEINBERG

38. FUSION ON FREIRE

His pedagogy, his ideological orientation, his exemplary life of service, his passion for living, his radical love, his humor, ad infinitum have made us better people and challenged us to a lifetime of engagement with the world around us. For these gifts I will always be profoundly grateful to Paulo.

Joe L. Kincheloe, 2006

It is an honor to contribute to this book, and it is an honor to have personal memories of Paulo Freire. It is also humbling to know that this volume is dedicated to Joe L. Kincheloe, to his life dedicated to Critical Pedagogy and his efforts in creating a world of equity and empowerment. This chapter is a fusion of my words, Joe's words, and the words of beloved friends–all of us engaged in recalling the essential ways in which Paulo Freire's person and work informed our lives.

When Joe was offered a Canada Research Chair at McGill University in 2005, he was told he would have to write a significant grant to create a sustainable research centre. Without hesitation, he said he would create a project dedicated to Critical Pedagogy, in the names of Paulo and Nita Freire. Our experiences with Paulo were one and the same as our experiences with Nita. Partners in love, in teaching, in scholarship, and life, Paulo's work and Nita's work was wound from two strands into a thread which wound throughout our lives. In 2006, The Paulo and Nita Freire International Project for Critical Pedagogy was created in Montreal, Quebec. It was launched March 2008, with many of the authors in this book in attendance. By naming the project for both Paulo and Nita, Joe intended to underscore the depth of the partnership between Paulo and Nita. And by using Paulo's pet name for his beloved, Nita (her given name is Anna Maria), Joe wanted to engage the intimacy and radical love, which they so publicly shared.

To commemorate the opening of The Freire Project, we gathered interviews from teachers, students, and scholars to discuss the power of critical pedagogy and the impact of Paulo Freire's work. In this short piece, I have included parts of interviews with Deborah Britzman (db), Henry Giroux (hg), Ramon Flecha (rf), myself (ss), and Joe Kincheloe (jlk). The purity of these words continues to inform me, and has been included in a new short film, *Paulo and Joe: The Struggle Continues* (freireproject.org). I weave my own comments within the weft of the text.

...somebody had given me a copy of *Pedagogy of the Oppressed*–read the book, I stayed up all night–I felt my life had literally changed - *hg*

T. Wilson, P. Park and A. Colón-Muñiz (eds.), Memories of Paulo, 165–169.
© 2010 Sense Publishers. All Rights Reserved.

Fascinated with the politics of education, the ideological dimensions of educational practice, I was immediately drawn to Paulo. I knew that an important dimension of my relative lack of success in formal schooling had to do with the ideological frameworks I brought to the classroom in the conservative and reactive world of the American South of the 1960s and early 1970s. All of what I found exciting and emancipatory about liberation theology expressed itself in Paulo's work. One afternoon I found a reference to *Pedagogy of the Oppressed.* Much to my delight there was a never-checked-out copy of the book in the stacks. I began reading. The next thing I remember the lights were switched on and off as the library was closing for the night. I had been reading for hours with no sense of time, place, or the pain of my earlier encounter with education. - *jlk*

I don't know how to say it; it was a book that made a tremendous difference in the way I started to think. No one had ever really talked about the idea that education oppresses. - *db*

It was 1987 and I was assigned to do an analysis of *Pedagogy of the Oppressed.* I put off the assignment for far too long and had little time to read it and write the piece. At the time I didn't realize that finding time to read the book wasn't an issue....I couldn't put it down. - *ss*

I returned to my dorm room with the book. I imagined Paulo working with the Brazilian peasants, teaching them to read the word and the world, developing generative themes that connected education to their everyday lives. Reading deep into the night, I noted the scholars Paulo referenced: Marcuse, Fromm, Marx, Lukacs, Simone de Beauvoir, Fanon, Sartre, Husserl, Niebuhr, Pierre Furter, and others. In my youthful enthusiasm I promised myself that I would read all of these people. And in response to my professors' disdain of my ability to engage in the life of the mind, I vowed to know as much about the tradition Paulo learned from as I possibly could, and to connect it to my own egalitarian southern Appalachian ways of being. I believed I could be a transgressive scholar on my own terms. I could take my southern mountain sensibilities and with the help of liberation theology, Freirean liberatory pedagogy, the African American rhythm and blues idiom, the radical comedy of Monty Python to George Carlin and Richard Pryor, the rock spirit of Bob Dylan and John Lennon, radical revisionist historiography, and other discourses I would discover as time passed, I could fashion ways of seeing and being that were my own and that contributed to larger political change. - *jlk*

...to read what Paulo wrote spoke to me as a woman more than anything else, in fact, to me, at the time I read it, it was the greatest, most feminist piece of work I ever read. - *ss*

In the early 90s, angry marauding women screamed that Paulo's words were sexist. Indeed, he only used masculine pronouns. These wails were my first introduction to the essentialist left: voices who privileged their own oppression above the voices of others. It didn't take long for me to become alienated from many of these women, and I found myself in a strange position, as a young critical pedagogue, a feminist, and one who worked with, played with, and loved men as well as women. No one spent much time discussing linguistic nuances, and the obvious fact was that translating Portuguese into English in those days did not usually include a crash course in political correctness. In 1991, or so, Paulo spoke at the American Educational Research Association, and apologized for his "sexist" language. He said he had never meant to insult anyone and the translation was a casualty of Latin languages. Paulo loved women, he respected women, and his work with women has always spoken to the deep reverence he has for all people. Paulo was always disturbed how the left was divided by essentialism. I have had a front seat view of the nastiness and bitterness that often erupted from people who did not understand the tentative and fluid nature of Critical Pedagogy. Even now, after forty years, we are still subject to remarks that the philosophy is a "White man's" diatribe, that it is controlled by "rockstars," on and on. Unfortunately, many of these voices have affected the tenure, scholarship, and well-being of teachers and scholars who have attempted to find their way via the critical theoretical ways of seeing the world. And ironically, those who most ignore the field of Critical Pedagogy also ignore the amazing contributions of the women and non-White scholars and cultural workers who engage in it. None of us have ever claimed to have the right answer. Indeed, as we all know, with Freire, there are no answers...only more questions. Until this unfounded critique of Critical Pedagogy is buried, I fear that the Right basks in the Left's squabbling.

For Paulo, no issues were personal...the personal was a vehicle to begin to talk about the public. - *hg*

My good friend Donaldo Macedo arranged for Shirley and me to meet Paulo in Boston. We went to Paulo's favorite Portuguese restaurant. We bonded immediately, of course, because he was from the poorest area of Brazil and I was from the poorest area of the US. - *jlk*

The first class (with Paulo) I went to, everyone was afraid...he made us all feel very comfortable, calling us: 'my friend, my friend...' hugging people and so on, until we could have meaningful discussions with him—we were just talking, the entire seminar was just whatever was on our minds...that is what we talked about—one thing I remember about Paulo was that sometimes he talked about his depression, and how he dealt with it. Like many of us, if we are lucky enough, he went shopping. He was very dapper, he was very handsome and cared about his dress; he was very interested and very funny. - *db*

We had amazingly similar resonating stories about our childhood, and how we arrived at our ideological and pedagogical positions. To be with Paulo, and coming where I come from...not thinking I would ever have the chance to be around someone like Paulo Freire; his friendship, his mentorship, and his genius changed my life and so many lives. - *jlk*

I have never been around anyone who told a story the way Paulo could. - *hg*

I remember going to Henry's house for the first time in Ohio, and Joe and I went with him to his office. As we walked in the door, the first thing that I saw was a framed letter from Paulo to a younger Henry complimenting him on his work. Henry said that it was the most valuable thing he owned. This was Henry Giroux telling me about his mentor; it was humbling. Listening to Henry, Donaldo, Ramon, Antonia....so many people telling stories about Paulo, I am always struck at how much they smile and laugh when they tell anecdotes. Their voices get intimate, they lean forward, and they share a sacred, strangely mundane story about this man...this force.

> I met him for the first time in January 1988–spent almost a week, talked about many things...Paulo Freire did not provide us with a method, he provided us with an understanding of society and education, and mainly we could learn a lot from (disenfranchised) people. He taught us that that learning is a process of communication, it is not a hierarchy; that was an incredible thing to learn for me–there is a necessity to recreate a critical pedagogy in the moment...not to recreate Paulo Freire—Paulo Freire said we need science, but we also need passion. - *rf*

I must mention our friends at CREA, from The University of Barcelona: a group of amazing teachers and cultural workers, birthed from the Basque/Catalan/Anarchist resistances, and loved so deeply by Paulo. This group of unstoppable researchers/ teachers has worked in areas of critical pedagogy and cultural work since the 1970s. Engaged in creating literacy groups with the disenfranchised Roma people of Barcelona, one sees critical pedagogy in action in this city. Ramon's dearest friend/brother, was Jesus "Pato" Gomez. Pato was Basque, as is Ramon, and it doesn't take one long to know the passion and power of the Basque persona. Ramon and Pato were two of Paulo's favorite people in the entire world. He shared his love of football, food, and philosophy in loud, engaging meetings while in Spain. Paulo once remarked to Nita how much he loved Pato...he told her "I love Pato, I love how he loves to eat. I never trust anyone who doesn't love to eat."

> I recall one beautiful afternoon in Sao Paulo at Paulo and Nita's home having the chance to talk at length with Paulo about the similarity of our childhoods in the rural mountains of Tennessee and Recife in northeastern Brazil. I have written elsewhere of how our mutual love of beans—beans and rice for Paulo and beans and cornbread for me—symbolized our shared experience of growing up in poverty stricken areas of our two countries. After our bean bonding Paulo opened a bottle of Beaujolais to toast our love and semiotic understanding of brown beans. It might sound bizarre to the callous urbane sophisticate, but this was one of the most memorable moments of my life. We spoke of love, humility, writing, and the politics of football. Nita and Shirley laughed at the similarity of our ideology of sports—we labeled ourselves sports radicals. Speaking with Paulo in this and other situations always took me back to the context of my initial discovery of his work and the role in played in my bizarre Appalachian Trail to critical pedagogy. - *jlk*

My fondest memories of Paulo are those with Nita. It is impossible to imagine the two of them separate. Paulo knew Nita in Recife when she was a young girl in his school. They met many decades later, both widowed, and both fell in love with abandon, with passion. I have turned much of my work into a quest to discuss Paulo's notion of radical love. In the context of the critical and the cultural, I am working to blend Fromm's critical notions, Joe's thoughts about passion and spirituality, and Paulo's and Nita's ability to see the critical, the radical, and the passionate within everything we do. I see it as a never-ending circle, which will encompass alternate forms of intelligence, different plains of existence, and embracing the imperfect. In all honesty, I am luckier than I would have ever imagined. Nita and I still talk and marvel at the fact that we have loved and been loved by these two men of passion and integrity. It goes without saying, I would give all to be able to be writing this chapter with Joe.

> And then he began speak of Nita...I was curious to know what she was like. And as his eyes got bigger and bigger, he talked about Nita and what he decided was definitely radical love—and then he started to historicize his own radicality, and how he had come to be a liberation theologist; how he had become a Marxist, and how he had become a teacher. And then he took it, and began to talk about how he bridged it and how he felt love for people and his career...and how his relationship with Nita was the culmination of everything. - *ss*

And I knew that moment, that that was radical love, and that was what I had with Joe.

REFERENCES

Cucinelli, G., & Smith, D. (2009). Producers. In *Paulo and Joe: The struggle continues*. Montreal: The Paulo and Nita Freire International Project for Critical Pedagogy.

Kincheloe, J. (2006). Introduction. In P. Freire (Ed.), *Teachers as cultural workers: Letters to those who dare teach*. Boulder, Co: Westview Press.

Pato, Paul, & Joe. (2009). *Film produced by The Paulo and Nita Freire International Project of Critical Pedagogy* (S. R. Steinberg, Producer; G. Cucinelli & D. Smith, Directors). Retrieved from freire project.org

Shirley R. Steinberg
Professora investigadora, Generalitat de Catalunya
Unversity of Barcelona
Director, The Paulo and Nita Freire International Project for Critical Pedagogy:
McGill University, Canada

EDITORIAL COMMENTARY

I began the task of polishing this book from an editor's perspective, with but a rudimentary knowledge of Paulo Freire. Approaching each of the contributions from the context of seeing that all was cited and formatted, I was nevertheless profoundly impacted by what emerged from this material. It allowed me an insider's view of a man whose influence on the profession of teaching is perpetual and immeasurable.

I have come to understand that Paulo Freire began a history-changing conversation. In the middle of an oppressive rhetoric that had continued unchallenged for generations, Freire started a new dialogue, with new terms and new ways of thinking about education.

Beginning with his exile from Brazil in 1964 and the subsequent publication of *Pedagogy of the Oppressed* in 1968 in Portuguese and 1970 in Spanish and English, Freire carried that conversation to North America and internationally, bringing countless others into the dialogue.

The pages in this book represent some of the powerful voices in the continuing threads of that conversation. These voices speak about a man who was a constant beacon for a radical paradigm shift in the field of education. Although he returned to live in Brazil in 1980 until his death in 1997, Freire had forged a philosophical collaborative that transcended geography. His impact, and his interactions, took place beyond borders. The reflections contained herein come from those who continue his work in the U.S., Canada, and elsewhere.

And yet, there is another picture of Paulo Freire that emerges, of just a man. He was kind, he loved food, he was full of life, and full of opinions. But, above all, he was faithful to the truths that he knew, and he never wavered from his mission of speaking those truths.

It is to the man, his teaching, and his faithfulness that this chorus of voices pays homage.

Patricia Harriman, Copy Editor
Memories of Paulo

AFTERWORD

A Fado for Freire

We are standing before the ignoble wreckage of a social order—a has-been state recycling second-hand ideas, where a politics of fear has been created, in part, by a bandying about of the term "terrorist" and an organic integration into the neoliberal state as internalized co-optation and forms of self-regulation resulting in a managed consent of the masses to their own domination. Such a turbid politics has stanched and fractured public debate on vexed political issues, quelling voices of dissent and proscribing public efforts at critical inquiry. The current administration's[1] contempt for civil rights has made a mockery of our constitutional system and defamed the historical struggle of social justice educators to create the conditions of possibility for students to become self-reflexive citizens.

The work of Paulo Freire constitutes an antidote to much of what is wrong with the current political landscape. Freirean _pedagogia libertadora_ is animated by a value-based vision of a better future for humanity through the development of a self-educative and transformative process that facilitates revolutionary praxis, a liberatory shaping of a collective political and ethical project. Interlinking critical theory, humanistic philosophy and the hermeneutic tradition of Marxist critique of political economy, Freirean pedagogy situates itself through dialogue and coope-ration—the conditions for the creation of _conscientizacao_. Through supporting the social development of individuals who are positioned as agents of history in the making, encouraging individuals and groups who are socially, culturally and econo-mically excluded, and intervening in both formal educational and non-formal educational settings, Freirean pedagogy continues to advance across the educational firmament.

He was a picaresque pedagogical wanderer, a timeless vagabond linked symboli-cally to Coal Yard Alley, to Rio's City of God, to the projects of Detroit and any and every neighborhood where working men and women have toiled throughout the centuries, a flaneur of the boulevards littered with _fruiterers_ and fish vendors and tobacco and candy stalls, the hardscrabble causeways packed with migrant workers and the steam punk alleys of dystopian dreams. This man of the people was as much at home in the _favelas_ as he was in the mango groves, a maestro who could cobble together the word and the world from the debris of everyday life, from its fury of dislocation, from the hoary senselessness of its cruelty, from its beautiful and frozen emptiness and wrathfulness of its violence. And in the midst of all of this he was able to fashion revolutionary hope from the tatters of humanity's fallen grace. This was Paulo Freire.

Some time ago in Lisbon, I went with a colleague to hear Joao Queiroz, an exponent of the Coimbra version of popular Portuguese music known as _Fado_ in a restaurant called _A Severa_ (named after Maria Severa, the intrepid gypsy singer who was the most famous interpreter of the Fado in the 19th Century). The word _Fado_ comes from the Latin and signifies fate or prophecy. Fado is meant to express various states of the soul–from melancholia, to happiness, to the satirical. Transfixed by the guitars and the majestic voice of the singer, I began to see this book as a type of literary Fado in honor of Paulo Freire. It is a Fado, yes, but it also has elements of José Alfonso's famous revolutionary song "Grândola, Vila Morena." It is a heart-rendering testament to the beauty and power of memory as Paulo's life and work are remembered and his love of the people and the comradeship–and revolutionary praxis–he developed with them are celebrated. We would do a disservice to Paulo to make him larger than life, because life for Paulo was larger than any one human being. But that should not stop us from imagining a Fado for Paulo, sung by Cristina Branca, and carried to the farthest reaches of our heart.

Because I spend a great deal of my time traveling internationally at the invitation of universities, teachers unions, and political and activist organizations, I am forced to do much of my writing in hotel rooms, airport lobbies and on dinner trays in airplanes. The writing of this afterword is no exception. Recently I gave a week of talks to elementary and secondary school teachers in Medellin, Colombia. One of the handful of schools that I visited during my visit to Colombia was *La Independencia*, a combined preschool, primary and secondary school (educacion preescolar, basica primaria y secundaria y media academia) located in the barrio of El Salado, sector de San Juan, comuna 13.

The school sits like an somber sentinel in the heart of comuna 13 where a massive military-police operation occurred in October 2002 (known as operation Orion), targeting members of the FARC (*Fuerzas Armadas Revolucionarias de Colombia* or Revolutionary Armed Forces of Colombia, established in the 1960s as the military wing of the Colombian Communist Party) and FARC sympathizers as well as members of the ELN (the National Liberation Army) and the CAP (People's Armed Comandos). On the orders of President Uribe, and led by the notorious General Mario Montoya, head of the army's Fourth Brigade and the man who led the scorched earth campaigns in Putumayo in 2001–2002), a combined task force of 3,000 army troops (mostly from the Fourth Brigade), intelligence agents, and police descended like a raging beast upon this shantytown of 100,000 people (many of whom are displaced Afro-Colombian peasants) in the central-western hill, with the backing of tanks and Blackhawk helicopter gunships that indiscriminately fired upon targeted areas. Young men were dragged out of homes, bound, and executed in front of horrified children. Targeting neighborhoods like 20 de Jilioi, Belencito, Corazon, El Salado and las Independencias, this "cleansing" operation that lasted twelve hours left 14 people dead and countless wounded. Hundreds of residents were arrested and at least 46 people "disappeared" in the immediate aftermath of the operation. Not long after the operation, the rightwing death squads of the AUC (United Self-Defence of Colombia, the feared paramilitary that succeeded Pablo Escobar in controlling Medellin's storied drug trade), most notably the Bloque Metro and Cacique Nitibarra, successfully supplanted the left-wing militants, and ruled the area by means of a bloody reign of terror. Most of the *milicianos* fled to Santa Ana, San Luis and Granada, in the northeastern part of the city. I was shown by the principal of La Independencia, pictures of the dead and dying and people holding white sheets who were shouting for the violence to stop.

Comuna 13 was not only known for its armed resistance to state terror, it was an area where residents excelled in organizing and building roads, schools, youth centers, and senior citizens' clinics with their own hands. The principal of La Independencia was proud of the accomplishments of the people of Comuna 13, and was determined after Operation Orion to help his students and their families heal, both physically and emotionally. He and his staff have taken a principled position to keep out of the school all illegally armed groups, including the FARC and the paramilitaries. The school sees its mission as keeping the students and teachers alive, nurturing them affectively and providing spaces of hope that can motivate them to seek enrollment in universities when they graduate. It has become a place of refuge and love (*amor al niño y refugio del niño*). While the school has taken a neutral position in the civil war (if it took a strong social justice position, teachers and administrators would almost certainly be assassinated), it has not abandoned the principle of solidarity with the oppressed. This is a courageous stand in the country with such a US-backed repressive state apparatus, where the military and its allied death squads wage a clandestine war against social movements and trade unionists. More trade unionists are assassinated in Colombia every year than in any other country.

In this school located on the razor's edge of human strife, I found the perfect place to reflect with the principal and the staff upon the importance of the work of Paulo Freire. Whenever I am in Latin America, Europe, Asia, or elsewhere, it is the name Paulo Freire that cements our passions together in a common struggle for justice.

While they have not suffered the fate of the youth in La Independencia, many of today's urban youth in the United States have had little to look forward to other than a life lived in the boulevard of broken dreams, ensepulchred within a granitic horizon of hopelessness that misery has rejected and even despair has abandoned.

We live in a world saturated by injustice. We cannot act justly by refashioning ourselves in an orgy of self-help voluntarism. We need to transform ourselves, yes, but through rebuilding the world in which our acts of justice take place. Our acts must eventually escape the framework of social relations in which they are encased. The circumstances in which people live need to be changed, yes, but it is the people who need to change them. This "change in circumstances" cannot be a gift bestowed by "those in the know" to those who know less. It is the people themselves who need to remove all obstacles to the full development of human beings–that is, after all, what the path to socialism is all about. We are talking here about the development of human capacities and human powers–in short, human agency–and the development of these not just for some select few but for all. This means self-management, co-management, co-operation, joint participation and collective development–all part of a protagonistic, participatory democracy. Michael Lebowitz (2008) affirms that this is what Marx meant when he talked about the concept of revolutionary practice–"the coincidence of the changing of circumstances and of human activity or self-change." All production should be about producing human beings. Factories, for instance, should be as much about producing human beings as producing commercial products. Lebowitz (2008) writes: "Through revolutionary practice in our communities, our workplaces and in all our social institutions, we produce ourselves as 'rich human beings'—rich in capacities and needs—in contrast to the impoverished and crippled human beings that capitalism produces."

A new world requires new social beings, but new social beings who are actively working to transform the world. I am reminded of Prince Myshkin, in Dostoevsky's masterpiece, *The Idiot*, who was a model of innocence in a world permeated by evil, but whose goodness sparked new acts of evil. In our world of faceless bureaucrats who control the courts and banks and Pentagon and mercenary companies and corporations and mass media, those who legitimize extraordinary rendition, water boarding and other forms of torture either by their ideological advocacy or by their stone silence, we are also reminded of Hannah Arendt's storied insight that the most unprepossessing and innocuous-seeming functionaries–those without the obvious political horns and tails–can commit the most atrocious of crimes. The more that evil is able to cohabitate with us unsuspectingly through the blind and mechanistic actions of model bureaucrats, primitive patriots and crass careerists, and the more that we permit evil to live frictionless in our midst, the less we recognize its malevolent presence and the more we begin to become evil ourselves. The inability of much of today's garden variety critical pedagogy–especially the domesticated and politically drained versions that fleck the landscape of our urban classrooms–to comprehend the nature and the extent of the alienation of today's youth has produced its inevitable result on the reconceptualization of the problematics that inform the meaning of education as non-oppression, that is, as liberation.

What about those who call themselves Freirean educators but whose actions bespeak anti-Freirean principles and practices? Recently, during a trip to the Universidade do Minho, in Braga (the fifth largest city in Portugal), I became aware of a puzzling and shameful situation. One of the professors there–a brilliant and well-published educational theorist, prominent social activist and popular teacher–is facing what can be straightforwardly called "social fascism." A group of academics–some of them laudably self-nominated *freireanists* and *left intellectuals*, using such terms no doubt to enhance their social mobility–are not only explicitly blocking and positively boycotting several events that he has been organizing–inviting noteworthy critical scholars from around the world to participate as key note speakers–but also declining to renew the approval of his research project (that has been approved since 2004), claiming that he has no legitimacy to work within the field of educational policy. Moreover they had the temerity to claim and stipulate that race, class, gender and sexual orientation were issues that have nothing to do with curriculum. The following is an excerpt from an official letter addressed to this professor:

> [We] have nothing to do with what you are reading or with your research, if you publish material here in Portugal or elsewhere related to Educational Policy. We have nothing against the fact that you are associated with this person, or that person. Do what you want. We will be here to judge and to evaluate what you are doing, and if you are doing appropriate work. However, you are not allowed to do what you are doing here at the Institute. Listen, what

you are doing has nothing to do with curriculum. I am sorry. You have to understand that once and for all. That is not curriculum. Issues of class, race, and gender and sexual orientation have nothing to do with curriculum. You are not allowed to work on those issues here at the Institute. [1]

This is pure societal fascism. What about academic freedom? What about the role of the university professor as a public scholar, a public intellectual? Such hypocrisy represents conditions in which educators (often careerists) talk left but walk right. Clearly, we need to clean up the Augean stables of critical pedagogy.

Paulo Freire has been at the center of almost every debate concerning the production and reproduction of the subject in modern and postmodern sites of learning and teaching. His legacy is daunting and his spirit indefatigable, his work foundational and ineradicable. There is a redivivus character to his thinking that gives his message an uncanny timelessness. No single educator has had such a singular purchase on the hearts and minds of generations of progressive educators throughout the world. It is no exaggeration to say that we can accept Freire or reject Freire, but we cannot, and must not, forget Freire. This is a book about remembering Freire. It is a series of heartfelt reflections on the humanity of Paulo Freire, on the ways that Freire's personality and pedagogical spirit have affected–and profoundly transformed–educators and activists worldwide, not to say impacted the very mission of education throughout the past thirty years.

Paulo Freire has much to say to today's teachers whose personalities seek nourishment and a chance to put down roots in a more secure pedagogical ground. His work cannot be transplanted, as if it were a static compendium of pedagogical insights. Rather, it needs to be treated as a process that is always in the making and that must be reinvented in the contextual specificity of where educators take up their particular challenge of teaching and learning. But critical pedagogy cannot be seen as a method, it is a way of being-in-the-world, and must be felt in the occult being of the teacher, in her or his self-sentient nature, by recognizing the sanctity of human life and of nature and the hidden history of otherness contained therein. For Freire, as for many revolutionary critical educators, praxis aggregates our political agency–and its differences–to collective struggle. Here critical pedagogy constitutes the building blocks for a relation with other people. In so doing, revolutionary praxis helps hope resume its odyssey of struggle against the obstacles of fear, ignorance and self-doubt.

Paulo Freire and I shared many moments together, both in North America and in his home in Brazil. He was a dear friend and mentor, and on one occasion in São Paulo during a grindingly academic speech of mine, he helped translate some of the most difficult words. And while he was always operating in an impossible schedule that had him in constant motion around the world, he still found time to pen prefaces and forewords for numerous works by international scholars with whose pedagogical projects he felt a comradely affinity. Such was the generosity of Paulo. Recently I went into the Church of St. Nicholas in Talliin, capital of Estonia (formerly known as Reval), to see the famous Danse Macabre painting as depicted at the end of the 15th century by Bernt Notke (likely the renewal of an analogous painting in Lubeck dating from 1461). The painting represents the transience of life as we see Death defeating both the mighty and the weak. Everyone was made to dance with Death: the Preacher, the Pope, the Emperor, the Empress, the Cardinal, the King, and the Bishop. Freire's work for me offers the same instruction as Notke's great work: power and privilege and status are but transient affairs and all of us would do well to work as brothers and sisters in the common task of building a better future for all of humanity, and not just those who abuse their earthly rankings. Paulo wrote to me after the death of his first wife, Elza, and he was in very bad shape. But he was to find another love of his life—Nita–and we spent moments together rejoicing in his new-found joy and happiness. Paulo was one of a kind, a singular spirit in a complex world. And while there are those who aspire to be the most important exponents of his life and work, there will never be anyone who possesses the necessary instruments to measure the pedagogical footprints he has left on our planet. And we welcome the reflections of all of these wonderful authors and editors who recognize this, and who celebrate the depth and scope of Paulo's legacy.

NOTES

[1] Protocol correspondence. (2007) Requerimento Enviado à Comissão Directiva do Centro de Investigação em Educação do Instituto de Educação e psicologia da Universidade do Minho, Braga, Portugal.

REFERENCES

Lebowitz, M. (2008) The Specter of Socialism for the 21st Century. This text is the keynote address to the annual meeting of the Society for Socialist Studies, Vancouver, June 5, 2008. It was originally titled "Building socialism for the 21st century". Links. http://links.org.au/node/503

Peter McLaren, Professor
Graduate School of Education and Information Studies
University of California, Los Angeles

BIBLIOGRAPHY

Freire, P. (2001). *Pedagogy of freedom: Ethics, democracy and civic courage*. New York: Rowman & Littlefield Publishers.

Freire, P., author. Oliviera, A., (Trans.) Prepared for publication by Freire, Ana Maria Araujo. *Daring to dream: Toward a pedagogy of the unfinished*. Boulder, CO: Paradigm Publishers.

The Pedagogy of the Oppressed, Paulo Freire's seminal book that was published in English in the U.S. first in 1970, has experienced several republications and numerous translations. In deference to the significance of that work, and toward a fair acknowledgement of each author's reference to it, the editors wish to cite here the breadth of its publication history in the U.S.:

Freire, P. (1970). *Pedagogy of the oppressed*. New York: Herder & Herder.

Freire, P. (1973). *Pedagogy of the oppressed*. New York: The Seabury Press.

Freire, P. (1986). *Pedagogy of the oppressed*. New York: Continuum.

Freire, P. (1993). *Pedagogy of the oppressed* (New rev. 20th-Anniversary ed.). New York: Continuum.

Freire, P. (2000). *Pedagogy of the oppressed*. New York: Continuum.

CPSIA information can be obtained at www.ICGtesting.com
Printed in the USA
LVOW10s1637250913

353756LV00011B/41/P